M000103662

I have given you a warp
of a light you do not know of.
I will have to give you some herbs
that will yield strange colours;
as heddles you will have to put
threads to be scented under the moon,
and you will have to weave a blanket
that, at my gallop, will open
like a flag
that men have never seen
and it will smell of our heaven
and the heart of our hills.
A blanket where my land
shall sing, shout, dance and cry!

Alfredo Bufano
To a weaver

The authors would like to thank Nicolás Bunge, Sergio Cazapa, Mario Cócolo, Mario Day, Nélida Teresa Donadío, Elisa Lester, Félix Namor, Jorge Quesada, Familia Ramallo, Pablo Rambozzi, Rodolfo Ramos, Marta A. de Rosa, Vivian Spoliansky, Delia Beatriz Taranto, Silvia R. de Tarasido and Tierra Adentro S.R.L. for their kind help.

Other books published by Maizal

Español/Spanish	*Inglés/English*	*Bilingüe/Bilingual*
El Mate	The Mate	Teatro Colón
El Tango	The Tango	Pintura Argentina/
El Gaucho	The Gaucho	Argentine Painting
Argentina Natural	Argentine Nature	
La Cocina Argentina	Argentine Cookery	
Carne Argentina	Argentine Beef	
Indios Argentinos	Argentine Indians	
Vinos Argentinos	Argentine Wines	
Textiles Argentinos		

Argentrip
Argentina's on-line travel guide
www.argentrip.com

© Enrique Taranto y Jorge Marí, 2003
Book and Cover Design: Christian le Comte y Sophie le Comte
Hecho el depósito que marca la ley 11.723
Las reproducciones están condicionadas a fin exclusivamente
didáctico y orientativo de esta obra (art. 10, Ley 11.723).
ISBN 987–9479–16–5, Buenos Aires, Argentina
Editado por Maizal Ediciones
Muñiz 438, B1640FDB, Martínez
Buenos Aires, Argentina.
E–mail: info@maizal.com
Impreso en noviembre de 2003 por Morgan Internacional.

Enrique Taranto
Jorge Marí

Argentine Textiles

MAIZAL
EDICIONES

Pre–Hispanic Weaving

Contrary to what the Europeans believed in 1492, that the American continent was peopled only by savages, the existence of centres of aboriginal civilization with outstanding features of cultural progress, awaited the conquerors.

Pre–Inca woven fabric with band tassels, Chancay, Peru

In South America, the Inca Empire was the bright beacon of civilization and from what today is Peru and down the Andean corridor, its customs and culture were radiated to north, east and south.

Textiles were present in all kinds of Inca ceremonies, they were offered as tributes to their monarchs and as presents to their warriors and high ranking officials, they were also used as elements of religious sacrifice and funeral rites.

Part of the territory of the Argentine Republic (the provinces of Tucumán and Catamarca), belonged to

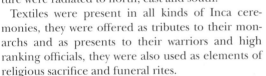

the Kollasuyo, the southern region of Tahuantinsuyo. Tahuantinsuyo was the name given to the Inca Empire, a word in Quechua language which means "the four parts".

Piece of pre–Inca cloth southern coast of Peru

The other three parts were the Chinchasuyo (the north) the Antisuyo (the east) and the Cuntisuyo (the west).

The provinces of Alto Peru (what today is Bolivia) formed part of the Kollasuyo and the Antisuyo, and made up the territory of the United Provinces of the Río de la Plata, the original name of Argentina.

Map of the four regions of the Inca Empire (Tahuantinsuyo)

In pre–Inca time, in the period that goes from 1500 BC to 1200 AD, this region was the site of the Tihuanaco culture. This area included the northern part of the Argentine province of Jujuy.

The collapse of Tihuanaco — still without explanation — allowed other ethnic tribes that had inherited their cultural characteristics to flourish. Among them were the Aymara Domains, which were independent groups linked only by a common language, the Aymara language. Constant struggles among them paved the way for their incorporation to the Inca Empire. When the Spaniards arrived the Incas were at the peak of their expansive splendour, which had started in 1430 under the reign of Tupac Inca (Pachacutec). The conquerors' arrival interrupted the Inca expansion.

Pre–Incan "unku", southern coast of Peru

The first remains of spun hand twisted fibres, found in Argentina are much older. The discovery was made in the Huachichocana Cave in the department of Tumbaya in the province of Jujuy and the textiles belong to the period that went from 6720 to 7670 BC From Inca Cueva in Humahuaca, also in Jujuy, other fabrics from around 2130 BC were found.

"Owl", Paracas 500–200 BC

"Double–headed snake", Paracas 500–200 BC

Textiles of similar antiquity were discovered in the Province of San Juan (in the Morrillos Cave, Department of Calingasta) and Mendoza (Indian Cave, Department of San Rafael). They had been spun with vegetable fibres plaited together with wool and human hair.

"Bird", Chimu, (1200–1450)

"Anthropofmorphic design", Chancay (1000–1450)

From the Early Period (500 BC to 500 AD) no relevant items have been discovered so far. Whereas the great amount of items have been found in Salta, belong to the Middle Period (500 AD to 1000 AD) and were woven by the Candelaria culture.

"Sea God", Inca, (1300–1530)

From the year 1000 on, in the Late Period, agriculture and cattle raising were developed in Salta and Jujuy. This gave these primitive inhabitants enough free time to devote themselves to textile art.

Piece of pre–Incan cloth with band tassles, southern coast of Peru

The Conquest

José del Pozo, "Patagonian woman", 1790

José Sánchez Labrador, S. J. (1717–1798) "Cotton or Mandiyú"

Sebastián Gaboto (1476–1557), the Genoese sailor in service to Spain, found Indians wearing ponchos, when navigating the Paraná upriver in 1529.

Ulrich Schmiedl, a Bavarian soldier and chronicler formed part of the expedition led by Pedro de Mendoza, who had come to found Buenos Aires in 1534. Schmiedl is the first to describe the Indians of the province of Buenos Aires. He maintains that the Charrúa and Querandí women were dressed in some sort of skirt in Buenos Aires and in Santa Fe: "These Indians [Charrúas] go stark naked, but the women cover their private parts with a small piece of cloth made of cotton, that goes from the navel to the knees. [...] These other women [Querandíes] wear a small cotton cloth covering only their private parts".

In Tucumán the natives wore garments made of lama wool.

The information about the clothes of the Indians of the southern region of the Pampas, leads us to think that they wore *quillangos* (pieces of leather sewn together) and that the spread of the use of the poncho happened much later. But if we go by a letter that Juan de Garay (second and definite founder of Buenos Aires) sent to the Spanish King in 1580 describing the Atlantic Coast of the Province of Buenos Aires, we can deduce that the Indians in the south used ponchos at the time of the Conquest. "There are great amounts of seals, and the people keep warm with blankets made of the skin of animals such as hares and wild cats and they build their tents with deer skins. We found some garments made of very good wool. They say that they bring them from the other side of the Andes."

The introduction of sheep by the Spaniards together with the cultivation of cotton in the Argentine territory was a transcendental contribution to the needs of the weavers. In 1556, cotton seeds were taken to the provinces of Santiago del Estero and Tucumán. Although the importation was made from Chile (La Serena), the seeds probably came from the Valley of Piura in Peru, where cotton was being intensely cultivated.

The Spaniards also insisted in the organization of the production and trade of woven material. In this task the religious institutions excelled, in 1587 thirty carts loaded with bundles full of textiles woven in Tucumán, ordered by their first bishop, the Portuguese Dominican Fray Francisco de Vitoria, arrived in Buenos Aires and were shipped to Brazil.

The Company of Jesus, in their workshops called "obrajes", in the missions, promoted spinning and weaving from 1609 on, until they were expelled in 1767.

These efforts bore fruit in all the regions of the country and from then on to present days, weaving is the most widespread and preserved craft in which both the aboriginal as well as the European traditions came together. The weavers in the northwest are mainly mestizos (of Spanish and Indian origin), those of Chaco and Patagonia are of pure Indian origin.

The tribes from the south traded their fabrics without middlemen even in war time. They went to the stores along the frontier to barter handicrafts for their vices: tobacco, yerba, sugar and liquor.

Emeric Essex Vidal (1791–1861) "Shop"

The Materials

Before the Spaniards introduced sheep rearing in Argentina, the natives of the American Southern Cone (the primitive ethnic groups that inhabited the Andean corridor) used wool from the American cameloids, to weave their textiles.

In Peru and even more in Bolivia, the weavers still use alpaca wool (*Lama pacos*), whereas the demand of llama wool (*Lama glauca*) and guanaco wool (*Lama guanicoe*) has diminished. The wool of the vicuña is reserved for the most valuable and finest items. In the northwest of Argentina,

Pre–Incan cultures of the Peruvian coast

vicuña is used only for the high quality items woven in Catamarca. In the south, along both sides of the Andes, where guanaco wool was used before the arrival of the Spaniards, sheep's wool replaced it in the nineteenth century.

If we examine an old poncho, *lliclla* (rectangular garment formed by two cloths sewn in the centre) or a *faja* (sash) from Alto Peru, we can observe that its fineness and quality is usually superior to the quality of the items woven in the south, both in Argentina and Chile.

This fineness, obtained by the thinness and torsion of the wool used, together with an exceptionally tight weaving, give the textiles a texture and a finish which resemble fabrics made of vegetable fibres and they look as if they had been woven in industrial looms.

M. de Frezier, "Working in a mine" Perú, siglo xviii

Vicuñas and guanacos still live in freedom today. The llama and the alpaca, the other two cameloids that live in the Altiplano, have grown accustomed to living with humans and have become domestic animals.

Martinez Companón, (1735–1797) "Indian shepherd"

In ancient times, the vicuñas were shorn from April to July and then freed again so that they could overcome the stress of the manipulation and be able to breed.

Only after three years, they were shorn again, to give the wool the possibility to grow again.

When the Spaniards arrived, they realized that this native system took a lot of time and started killing the vicuñas with their harquebus. The natives soon followed the bad example and the vicuñas were put on the verge of extinction.

Llamas transporting salt

"Before the Spanish conquest, there were 3 million vicuñas. In 1965 there were only 10.000 left.

Distributed in Argentina, Bolivia, Peru and Chile, today there are around 200.000 vicuñas, 37.000 of them are in Argentina." (Vilá)

There is strong evidence that in 6000 BC the camel-oids of the Altiplano were already domesticated but the practice of intensive shepherding took place at the beginning of the eleventh century, at least around the Titicaca lake, where there is a strong concentration of these species.

Caraguatá shirt, Chaco, nineteenth century

Caraguatá or cha-guar is a plant of the Bromeliaceae family, the leaves of which are used to produce a thread similar to hemp.

In order to dye, the weavers needed white wool and white wool was difficult to get, this was especially the case with alpaca wool. After the Spanish conquest, most of the weavers adopted sheep's wool. Sheep's wool is normally white.

Andean weavers did not reject anything that could be of some help; that is the reason why cotton should also be mentioned in connection with the manufacture of cloth.

Although the intensive cultivation of cotton in Argentina was started by the Spaniards, cotton is a native American plant and was thus known by the Indians who also knew how to cultivate it long before the conquerors' arrival.

Cotton yarn was used in Inca tapestry, and even before, by the cultures that had flourished in the coast of Peru between the first and eighth centuries such as Paracas, Nazca and Huari. Cotton was also found as weft in textiles, in regions like Tarabuco (Bolivia), where it was mixed with wool, which gave the cloth a very special touch because of the difference in texture.

Alpaca (Lama pacos)

In the workshops of the Jesuitical missions, cotton was also used; it was even combined with sheep's wool or any cameloid wool.

In the template zones of the north of Argentina and in Paraguay, cotton textiles, especially ponchos made of cotton, are very common. In the regions where the Chaco and Guaraní Indians live, there are many items, sashes, bags and shirts woven with another vegetable fibre, they are manufactured with *caraguatá* (in Quechua language "*chaguar*").

Llama (Lama glama)

In connection with the introduction of sheep in Argentina, William Mac Cann, an English traveller, made o vivid description of what he had seen in 1847. He wrote that from the moment he had left Buenos Aires, he had crossed many farms that devoted themselves to sheep breeding, in reality, he insisted, the whole countryside around the city devotes itself to sheep rearing.

Guanaco (Lama guanicoe)

How did this start? It all began with the arrival of Don Ñuflo de Chávez to Asunción del Paraguay with a herd of sheep that he had taken from Peru in a legendary expedition, in 1548 or 1549.

Some say that these sheep descended from the animals that Juan de Garay had taken with him in 1573, when he left Asunción in order to found the city of

Vicuña (Vicugna vicugna)

C. E. Pellegrini
(1800–1875)
"Don Juan Harratt,
breeder of merino
sheep in the Río de
la Plata"

Martinez Compañón,
(1735–1797)
"Indians sheep
shearing"

Santa Fe and in 1589 when he founded Buenos Aires for the second time. William Mac Cann, on the other hand, wrote that the sheep in these provinces descended from those introduced in 1590 by Juan Torres de Vera y Aragón, who, in order to fulfil an obligation he had with his father in law Juan Ortíz de Zárate, brought four thousand sheep from Charcas which then spread in the Provinces of Buenos Aires, Santa Fe and Corrientes.

These sheep belonged to a poorer breed called *churra*, the most ordinary breed in Europe. They were high, had straight wool, a long head and their face and paws were hairless.

The merino breed, which has a better wool quality, was not brought to America because Spain did not want the colonies to compete with her own production.

Two hundred years went by until the Spaniards living in the colonies started a movement against what they considered a great injustice.

Action was taken by the Marquis of Campomanes in 1774 and the Viceroy Loreto in 1790 arguing that if the colonies started producing and exporting wool and cloth, the Crown would benefit from it, but their efforts failed and the prohibition was not lifted.

In 1794 the Argentine poet Manuel José de Lavardén (1754–1809) succeeded in introducing a herd of merino sheep. Up to then, Argentina had two o three million animals, but they were of very poor quality. They all descended from the ugly *churra*, and they had developed into two different types: the *criolla*, small and with scarce wool and the *pampa*, a bit bigger and with better wool.

In 1814, the North American consul Thomas Lloyd Halsley imported another herd of thirty five merino animals and to guarantee the success, he hired the German shepherd Otto Dewahagen. These sheep were the first high quality animals that entered Argentina. They were taken to the farm "Los Altos de

Juan León Pallière, (1823–1887) "Weaver from Santiago del Estero"

Halsley" in what is today Moreno in the province of Buenos Aires. He obtained good results and, in 1819, he already had four hundred animals. Unfortunately a fire ended the enterprise, only thirty animals survived.

It was the first Argentine president, Bernardino Rivadavia (1780–1845), who laid the foundation for high quality sheep breeding and the refinement of the different breeds from 1824 on. This practice started a continuous progress which impelled the development of many other important activities in the young country.

Churra

Year after year, the grass–eating sheep displaced the rough cattle southwards. This happened at a rate of about 15 km a year and the farmers accompanied the movement. Even the villages moved southwards and many people went to live in the country where manpower was required.

Merino

Sheep rearing also gave the farmers the impulse to fencing off their farms and meat–processing plants

Juan León Pallière,
(1823–1887)
"Shearing"

*"They also make
cojinillos dyed in
blue or black. They
are made of poor
quality cloth in
which they introduce
fine pampa wool.
The thread has to be
between 25 and 30
cm long.
The Indians are very
keen on getting this
type of yarn and the
difficulty is one of
the reasons of the
high prize they get
for their work.
"The woven fabrics
of the Pampa
Indians are extreme-
ly resistant and that
is the reason for their
being difficult to
find."*
E. Kermes

*José Aguyari
(1843–1885)
"Shearing"*

started their activities, the first ship-
ment to Europe was a consignment
of frozen rams.

Enrique Kermes wrote in 1893:
"The only textile fibre used by
Pampa Indians is guanaco wool,
and since the introduction of
sheep, sheep's wool. Now they use
exclusively sheep's wool, because guanacos tend to
disappear.

For the production of ponchos and chiripáes (sort
of shawls, the two ends of which are fastened with a
sash round the waist, the middle part hanging down
like a bag and forming a kind of very loose trousers),
wool from the pampa sheep is preferred; the ponchos made with this type of wool are practically water-
proof. For saddle–blankets merino sheep's wool is
chosen, because it is much softer."

Alfredo Taullard, a contemporary Argentine researcher and historian, explains how the Mapuche
families kept sheep herds, "The sheep brought by
the Spaniards degenerated as time went by, forming
a breed that the Araucano Indians call *ofija* (corruption of the word *oveja*, Spanish for sheep) with long
and thick wool.

After leaving the wool untouched for some time,
they proceed to untangle the threads and start carding it carefully, combing and stretching the wool into
parallel and regular strips to ease the process of spinning."

The Araucano Indians were very meticulous in the
preparation of their textile fabric, of their famous
and beautiful ponchos and their warm blankets.

Spinning

One day, a girl was washing mote (cooked and peeled corn or wheat) in the river, when an old man came and stole it. He told her that he was going home and that he would return and that in the meantime, the girl had to spin wool.

Anonimous, "The Virgin, spinning" Cuzco, seventeenth century

The old man went away and the girl was left crying, she did not know how to spin. She sat by the fire with her sorrow, when all of a sudden, the Choñowe Kuzé (the old fire) spoke: "You don't have to be upset; I'm going to call Lalén Kuzé (the old spider)".

When the spider came, she said: "You have to imitate my work, look at me and you will learn to spin".

Days went by, and when the old man returned, the wool was spun. Lalén Kuzé had gone every night to help the girl and finished the task. (Montecino)

European spindle, nineteenth century

The magical–mythical beliefs of the Mapuche religion have influenced all aspects of their life and this legend is a proof of it.

Silk–threads are often tied around the wrist of new born girls or small spiders are made to walk in the palms of their hands, because it is believed that the spider will transmit the secrets of the most important element in textile art: the thread.

For the Mapuche Indians everything that has to do with weaving belongs to the feminine environment, this is not the case in the Altiplano, where the whole family weaves, including men.

In his *Comentarios Reales* Garcilaso de la Vega wrote: "The Indians liked weaving and hated losing their time. While going to and fro, or when paying their visits, they always took with them the utensils they needed to either spin or twist the yarn. In some remote places, far from Cuzco, which were not well tended by the Inca kings, women went to work in the field while men stayed at home and spun and wove."

Fausto Burgos and María Elena Capullo after years of intense research in Cuzco and the Argentine northwest, wrote in their book *Inca and Criollo Textiles* that they had seen many men who descended from Incas and Kollas, spinning with the spindle and going to and fro naturally, free from any anxiety, as if they were playing.

The process of obtaining wool has to be explained before the spinning method. If the wool is shorn, then the process of separating the wool from the leather has already been done. When a wild animal is hunted or has fallen into a trap, then the weaver gets the wool together with the skin. In that case, the Indians burry the skin in a wet place for several days, for the hide to rot. When it is dug up, then the weaver has only to seize the tufts and she will obtain the wool.

From Mendoza to Peru this was the common practice with the hide of the cameloids.

In the case the weaver got the fleece, if it was going to be a fine piece, then the fibres from the different parts of the body of the animals were separated according to characteristics and colour (in the case of the vicuña, back, belly and flanks). Then the wool was carded.

The weaver took a tuft, and evenly separated the fibres which she piled in a bag, on a piece of cloth, or on her own apron, that usually had a pocket to put the carded wool in.

When she had finished, she got her spindle, called *kulíu* in Mapuche language, *puchsca* in Quechua and *capuz* in Aymara.

Spindle

Whorl

Aspahue
(skeiner)

The spindle is a 25 cm long stick slightly sharpened at one end with a balancing whorl at the bottom. This whorl is a disk with a hole in the centre made of stone, wood, or ceramic to give it the necessary weigh and favour the turning.

Burgos points out that he saw an old man in Atuel, using a fig raisin as a whorl which was crossed in its centre by a small stick.

Its name in Mapuche language is *chinked*; in Quechua, *piruro*; in Catamarca, Santiago del Estero, Salta and La Rioja they call it *muyuna* (in Quechua, *muyuy* means to turn).

Taking a wisp of a ball of natural wool or hair, the weaver will wind it around her left wrist, holding it between thumb and index; she will stretch the tip with her right hand, matching the fibres and form a yarn. Then she will tie it to the spindle and with her hand she will turn the spindle clockwise, as if it were a top turning in the air.

Nicolás Rubió, "Spinning in Illimani", 2003

The yarn has to be as long as possible, and the spinner then winds it on the fingers of the left hand and then immediately on to the spindle, to form a small ball. Then the procedure is restarted.

When the ball is big enough, she leaves it and starts a new one. She can use another spindle and whorl, or she takes off the whorl and puts is on another spindle or as a third possibility, she can make a ball with the spun wool and use the spindle again.

The spinning wheel moved by a treadle was brought from Europe by the Spaniards and was widely used by the people in America.

It formed part of every household in colonial times.

Nicolás Rubió, "A mother in Huaylas", 1994

José Sánchez Labrador, S. J., (1717–1798) "Spinning"

The yarn obtained is of a single strand, and for the wool to be resistant and elastic it must have at least two strands. So a second bigger spindle called *kanti* by the Quechuas and *ckapu kanti* for the Aymaras is taken.

Tying two ends of the same yarn, she makes the spindle turn, this time counter clockwise, thus being able to form a yarn of two strands (Z–spun and S–plied).

Fray Diego de Ocaña, (c 1570–1608) "Araucanian Indian"

The yarns used in the Argentine and Chilean south are thicker than those used in the north, but the finest and most delicate ones are only found in Peru and Bolivia. In these countries even a third step is taken, which is called over–spinning. This two–strand yarn, which has already "relaxed", is forced to twist back on itself. This over–spinning is responsible for the thin and smooth quality of Bolivian textiles.

European spindle, nineteenth century

Lastly we will refer to a special technique that has been used for several centuries in Peru and in Alto Peru. It has not only a ritual meaning but it will give the fabrics of exceptional quality, a high resistance along the borders.

As it has already been explained, when a yarn is spun clockwise (to the right), we say that it is Z–spun and S–spun when it is done counter clockwise (to the left).

The yarn is usually Z–spun and S–plied but in very special items, the pairing of S–spun and Z–plied warp threads (forming half centimetre wide fringes) is used. A zigzag is then created, which has the effect of a herringbone, called by the Indians "fishbone".

Lloque, detail

In pre–Hispanic times in certain communities, only some very special people were allowed to weave in this way. Among Aymaras, the *lloque* (S–spun and Z–plied) was done by a dignitary, the *yatiri*, given the high meaning it implied.

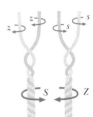

S and Z twisting

S and Z plied

Kipu, an Incan communication system

Dyeing

If we consider the extraordinary ability of the weavers in the development of the aboriginal cloth production, we cannot ignore the skill of these weavers in the process of dyeing.

Dyeing has been an interesting aspect of the development in all cultures. In old civilizations, the dyers have always formed part of the higher social classes. This happened not only in Asia but in Europe as well. Families of dyers zealously kept the secrets of their techniques that were only transmitted from one generation to the next, within the same family.

Although the arrival of the Spanish conquerors marked a turning point in the history and development of our continent, their influence was not enriching regarding dying techniques.

In 1040 BC, the Paracas culture in the northern coast of Peru had already produced a wide range of more than a hundred shades of different colours of quality and definition similar to those the Romans had achieved with Greek and Asian dying techniques.

When the Spanish conquerors had the opportunity to appreciate the rich, lively and bright Aztec and Inca fabrics, they were amazed at the colours they had achieved. In their chronicles they described these marvellous garments, putting special emphasis on the advantages of their organization in the production and commercialisation of dyestuff.

The conquerors took advantage of this and started exporting large amounts of cochineal and indigo to Europe.

Hernán Cortés (1485–1547) "Nopal"

José Sánchez Labrador, S. J. (1717–1798) "Prickly pear"

Poncho from Alto Peru dyed with ground cochineal

Mapuche ring poncho

*System used to dye a
ring poncho*

Wool scales

For centuries trading dyestuff would become a highly profitable activity and the Europeans would be able to enjoy reds and blues they had never dreamt of before.

From its origins to the present day, the dyeing technology has undergone many changes, but undoubtedly, in essence, the dyeing method is still based on three pillars: the washing, the use of mordants and the soaking of textiles in the dye bath.

Fabrics can be dyed after having been woven, but with the exception of the famous Pampa ponchos with rings (the technique of which will be explained further on), there are no other applications in quality fabrics in Argentina in what concerns the dyeing of finished cloth. This is the reason why only the process of dyeing sheep, goat or cameloids (alpaca, llama, vicuña and guanaco) wool is described. Cotton and even *caraguatá* fibres, can also be dyed, but, although the colours obtained are the same, their shades and intensity vary considerably.

In order to avoid problems when dyeing, the preparation of the skeins is of crucial importance. If we want to achieve an even colour, the skeins must have approximately the same weight, be loosely wound and tied, and the threads have to be kept separate. We have to bear in mind that for the warp–ikat technique (*guarda atada*), we have to tightly tie a piece to prevent that specific part from being dyed.

*Martínez Compañón,
(1735–1797)
Processing wool*

Shepherdess near her hut

Shearing

Dyeing wool

Cleaning wool

Carding wool

Spinning

Preparing the warp

Cleaning wool

Spinning

Dyeing wool

Pressing wool

Weaving

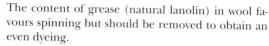
Washing

The content of grease (natural lanolin) in wool favours spinning but should be removed to obtain an even dyeing.

Water should be pure, the ideal, of course, is distilled water (ancient dyers and aboriginal weavers used rain water for the dyeing process). Hard water should be avoided.

To purify hard water, it should be boiled for quite a long time to allow the salts to decant. It is necessary to change the container as often as possible, because the salts will always decant on the bottom.

Quillay (Bredemeyera colletioides)

Nowadays, all Indian tribes from the Kollas in the north to the Mapuches in the south use modern soap powder but this was not so easy a hundred years ago. A century ago, the properties of certain vegetables with high contents of saponin were used. This substance contained in the fruit of the *quillo* (*Soleanum eleagnifolum*) and the bark of the *quillay* (*Bredemeyera colletioides*) not only removes the grease easily but has bleaching properties as well.

The Indians also washed their fabrics with *jume* ash, and the reason for that is worth explaining.

Jume, together with white *cachiyuyo*, grow in salty soils, thus absorbing high amounts of salt in their tissue. When jume is burnt, the action of fire frees carbon which combined with salt produces sodium carbonate. This soda ash obtained has a high cleansing power.

Quillo (Soleanum eleagnifolum)

With this ash aboriginals prepared the bleach used to wash their fibres.

There are two varieties of *jume*: *Allenrolfea vaginata* and *Suaeda divaricata*. Both bushes belonging to the *jume* family, do not look alike but have the same properties. With *jume* the Indians prepared a kind of soap, which was so good, that it even appeared as a possible American export item at the World Fair in Paris in 1867.

Although wool can be washed in cold water, it is better to put it in boiling water together with the detergents. Wool will not alter its physical aspect, if it is handled with care. If it is only gently moved, it will not become matted.

Once the wool has lost its lanolin, it should be rinsed in abundant water. In areas where there is water shortage or one is pressed for time, or it is necessary to save fuel, one can use the same water for the mordant process as for the dyeing.

Some dyers apply the mordant and then the dye, others do it at the same time, and still others use the dye and then the mordant.

*Jume
(Suaeda divaricata)*

*Martinez Compañón,
(1735–1797)
"Indians cleaning
wool"*

Use of mordant

*Martinez Compañón,
(1735–1797)
"Blue dyebath"*

Once the wool has been washed and the grease is removed, the process of dyeing can begin.

The function of mordants is to allow a better penetration of the dye into the fibre; it is also responsible for the fastness of the colours. It makes colours resistant to the action of light, water and rubbing.

Fermented urine is one of the most common elements used as mordant. Its active principles are urea and nitrogen components.

A simple mordant is kitchen salt (sodium chloride) and since it is usually kept at home, all aniline dyeing methods recommend the use of it. But one cannot rely on salt because the dye will not evenly penetrate the fibre and the colours will not be fast.

Alum (double aluminium and potassium sulphate), cream of tartar, soot, rust, acetic acid, vinegar (diluted acetic acid), *rovo* (earth with a high content of iron sulphate found in marshy soils) and even diluted sulphuric acid are excellent mordants.

In the whole country the wool was put in this bath before soaking it in the dyestuff. In the south, the Mapuche indians heated the water and then diluted the dye with the mordant.

Other substances are also used: *aloja* (a drink made of corn), and the bran of fermented wheat and bleach of *jume* ash, which has already been mentioned for its detersive properties, can be used as fixatives.

Another fundamental requisite for fast colours is the necessary amount of water: the more the better. The minimum proportion acceptable is 10 to 1, that is 10 litres of water for 1 kg of dry wool.

Dyeing

When the skeins are soaked in the dye bath, they have to be evenly wet; the dyestuff correctly diluted in water and the water has to be hot. The wool has to be left in the bath for a reasonable amount of time, at least an hour and it is advisable to leave it in the bath until it cools down.

A trick to enhance the shade of the colour is to rub ashes into the dyed wool so that it gets evenly impregnated and to soak it again in the dye bath.

The skeins have to be rinsed in clean water in order to remove unwanted substances.

Today, anilines have displaced all natural dyestuff, but this was already the case in 1927. Fausto Burgos writes: *"People dye with anilines in the places connected by the railway, which brings all novelties of civilization; primitive dyeing is only used in the regions the train does not reach…"*

Alzate y Ramirez, (México 1777) "Collecting cochineal"

Market in Casabindo, province of Jujuy. Anilin dyestuff

Natural cochineal

Ground cochineal

Dyed wool

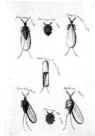

Nevertheless, it is important to mention the dye elements used by our aboriginal ancestors.

Certain vegetables have been described as "colour guardians", although one should not forget certain minerals such as iron oxide, which fixes and dyes in the grey gamut.

Among dyestuff, the seat of honour is for cochineal, the dried, pulverized bodies of certain female scale insects, *Dactylopius coccus*. This cactus–eating insect, native to tropical and subtropical America was one of the most important products exported from America.

The dye was introduced into Europe from Mexico where it had been used long before the arrival of the Spaniards. The cacti were the nopal in Central America and the prickly pear in Argentina.

When the National Exhibition of 1871 was organized in Córdoba, cochineal appeared in a report of natural resources sent by the Province of San Juan: *"cochineal (Coccus caota) is a native product from Valle Fértil and from Pedernal where the cactus that feeds this insect grows. The quality of it is extraordinary and it is as abundant as in the Provinces of Santiago del Estero and La Rioja. The harvest of it could easily be improved…"*

The other element that monopolized the attention of Europeans was indigo, a leguminous bush which is the raw material for a paste that produces blue colour. Its scientific name is *Indigofera suffructicosa Mill.* or *Indigofera kurtzii Harms* according to the variety found.

Both grew in subtropical and temperate zones and were used by Pampa and Araucano Indians from the Valley of the Río Negro and even in zones further south which comes to prove the intense trade within the American continent before the conquest.

Burgos writes:

Indigo stones

"*1. To make indigo extract one has to put crushed twigs of the indigo bush in barrels full of water. Stir constantly for the water to dissolve the dye substance. Then the twigs have to be taken out of the water and lime has to be added, leaving the preparation in contact with the air for the dye to precipitate.*

2. Without using mordants, put the fibre in indigo water or

Ground indigo

3. Use alum as mordant, put the dry threads in barrels containing urine for two or three days, take them out again and leave them in the open air, in the sun for a whole day. Rub them when dry and put them back in fresh urine for two days, adding a pouch of indigo, cook over low heat and remove the fibres to avoid burning, rub them again: iridescent steal blue."

Dyed wool

Plants Used as Dyes

Arranged according to resulting colour:

Canna indica

RED
Cochineal is not mentioned in this list because it is of
animal origin.
Puna Saffron *(Chuqiragua longiflora)*
Coronillo *(Scutia buxifolia)* fruit mixed with bark
Wild Porotillo *(Hoffmanseggia falkarina)*
Ceibo *(Erythrina cristagalli)* flowers
Achira *(Canna indica)* seeds
Socondo or Charrúas Roots *(Gallium hirsutum)*
Pellín Oak *(Nothofagus oblicua)* core without the bark
Relbún *(Relbunium hipocarpium, Hemsl)* roots
Quintral *(Lorantus sternbergianus L.)* flowers
Oxalidea *(Oxalis rosea)*

Scutia buxifolia

PINK
Palo de Santo Domingo or Tista–tista. *(Randia pubes-cens)*
Coshque Yuyo or Palta *(Maytenus vitisidaea)* roots
Laurel *(Laurus nobilis, Laurelia aromatica)*
Pellín Oak *(Nothofagus obliqua)* bark
Relbún *(Relbunium hipocarpium, Hemsl)* roots boiled
in sea water

*Hoffmanseggia
falkarina*

DARK SALMON
Lapacho *(Tabebuia araliacea)* sawdust, use without mor-dant, boil with a handful of soda ash

PURPLE
Piquillín *(Condalia lineata)* roots
Red Quebracho *(Quebrachia lorentzii)* sawdust
Meona Grass, Paiquillo, Ataco or Bledo *(Amarantus muricatus, Amaranthus quitensis)*
Cardón *(Cereus forbesi)* plant
Abriboca *(Centaurea melitensis)*
Mulberry *(Maclura mora)* fruits

Lorantus sternbergianus

VIOLET
Maqui *(Aristofelia chilensis)* plant
Palo Rosa *(Pterogyne nitens)* sawdust
Romaza *(Rumex romassa)* leaves and shafts
Red Poppy *(Papaver rhoeas)* flower

Laurus nobilis

ORANGE
Jume *(Spirostachys patagonica, Suaeda divaricata, Allenrolfea vaginata)* ashes mixed with Contrayerba.
Muermo or Ulmo *(Eucriphia cordifolia Cav.)*
Romaza *(Rumex romassa)* roots mixed with oak bark
Linquén *(Rocella tinctorea)*

Cereus forbesi

BROWN
Algarrobo blanco *(Prosopis alba)* resin contained in the bark
Algarrobo negro *(rosopis nigra)*
Visco *(Acacia visco)* bark
Walnut tree *(Juglans australis)* fruit bark

Papaver rhoeas

BRICK
Quintral *(Lorantus sternbergianus L.)* flowers
Muermo or Ulmo *(Eucriphia cordifolia Cav.)* bark

Aristotelia chilensis

BEIGE
Boldo *(Boldean fragans)* plant

Schinus dependens

YELLOW
Tola *(Hyalis spartioides)* mixed with urine
Pingo–pingo, Tramontana, Pico de Gallo or Pico de Loro *(Efedra tweediana)*
Toca del Norte or Sacha Huasca *(Bignonia family)* flowers
Quilcha Amarilla or Pichanilla *(Grindelia pulchella)*
Clavelilla *(Clavelillo Zinnia pauciflora)* flowers
Aguaribay *(Schinus molle)* leaves
Calafate or Quebrachillo *(Berberis ruscifolia, Berberis buxifolia)*
Red willow or *criollo* Willow *(Salix humboldteana)* bark
Barba de Piedra or Barba de Palo *(Usnea barbata)* the whole plant
Contrayerba, Valda, Chasca, Dauda *(Dorstenia contrayerba)*
Quejatulpuno *(Flaveria contrayerba)*
Puna Saffron *(Chiquiragua longiflora)*
Sweet Chilca *(Flourensia campestris)* with alum as mordant
Wild Camomile *(Anthemis cotula)*
Mora *(Maclura mora)*
Michay *(Berberis Congestiflora Darwin B.)* plant
Boldo *(Boldean fragans)* bark and leaves
Maitén *(Maytenus boaria)* sawdust
White Voqui *(Lardizabala biternata)* shafts
Lapacho *(Tabebuia araliacea)*, boiled sawdust
Coihue *(Nothofagus dombeyi)*
Lemon *(Citrus limonium)* clusters
Huellén *(Solidago microglossa)* flowers

*Berberis ruscifolia o
Berberis buxifolia*

Usnea barbata

Citrus limonium

BLUE
Indigo *(Indigofera añil, Indigofera suffructicosa Mill, Indigofera kurtzii Harms)* crushed clusters
Acacia *(Robinia pseudo–acacia)* leaves
Mata negra *(Atamisquea emarginata)* roots
Romaza *(Rumex romassa)* flower
Maqui *(Aristotelia chilensis)* fruits

LIGHT BLUE
Black Palque or Black Duraznillo, Hediondilla *(Cestrum parqui)* ripe fruits

Anthemis cotula

GREEN
Sweet Chilca *(Baccharis caliprinus)*
Jarilla *(Larrea divaricata)* crushed clusters
Indigo *(Indigofera añil, Indigofera suffructicosa Mill. Indigofera kurtzii Harms)* mixed with Contrayerba *(Flaveria contrahierba)*
Michay *(Berberis congestiflora Darwin B.)* leaves and shafts
Lingue *(Persea lingue)*, leaves and green branches
Laurel *(Laurus nobilis, Laurelia aromatica)* mixed with cinnamon
Cinnamon tree *(Drimys winteri)* crushed wood and leaves
Ñire *(Nothofagus antartica)* sawdust
Coihue *(Nothofagus dombeyi)* crushed leaves
Jume *(Suaeda divaricata, Spyrostachys patagonica)* roots mixed with alum
Tala *(Celtis espinosa, Celtis celowiana)* crushed wood, using urine as mordant
Palda blended with indigo
Tramontana *(Ephedra tweediana)* blended with orange juice or with indigo
Yerba Mate *(Ilex paraguaiensis)* leaves
Molle *(Duvava longifolia)* leaves blended with rust

Indigofera añil

Robinia pseudo–acacia

DARK BROWN

Mistol *(Zizyphus mistol)* bark and roots

Pelu *(Sophora tetraptera)* plant

Pelai *(Muhlenbeckia thamnifolia, Meisn)* crushed branches

Radal *(Lomatia obliqua)* bark

Lingue *(Persea lingue)* bark

Quintral *(Loramtus sternbergianus)* flowers mixed with maqui leaves *(Aristotelia chilensis)*

Chañar *(Geoffroea decorticans)* bark with alum as mordant

Espinilllo *(Acacia atramentaria, Acacia caven)* crushed wood with alum as mordant

Arrayán *(Eugenia uniflora, Luma apiculata)* bark

Lingue
(Persea lingue)

OCHER

Pitra *(Eugenia multiflora Hook)* crushed wood

Ulmo or Muermo *(Eucriphia cordifolia)*

Aguaribay *(Schinus molle)*

Citrus limetta

GREY

Molle de la Sierra or Molle incienso *(Duvava longifolia, Duvava latifolia)* roots

Quebracho *(Schinopsis lorentzi)* blended with iron sulphate

Bergamota *(Citrus limetta)* leaves boiled and blended with iron sulphate

Tusca, Aromo, Churqui or Espinillo *(Acacia cavenia)*

Granada *(Punica granatum)*

Chilco *(Fuchsia macrostema)* leaves

Lingue *(Persea lingue)*

Algarrobo blanco *(Prosopis alba)*

Atamisqui *(Atamisquea emarginata)* bark

Kitchen soot

Ulmo o Muermo
(Eucriphia cordifolia)

LEADEN

Nalca or Pangue *(Gunnera chilensis)* roots
Pangui *(Gunnera scabra , Urtica sp.)* roots
Pellín Oak *(Nothofagus obliqua)*
Chilca *(Baccharis calliprinus, Flourencia campestris)*
Romaza *(Rumex romassa)* leaves

BLACK

Quentitaco *(Prosopis adesmoides)*
Espinillo or Algarrobillo, Cebil, Sacha Cebil or Horco *(Atramentaria, Piptademia communis, Parapiptadenia excelsa)* bark with iron sulphate
Guayacán negro *(Caesalpina melanocarpa)*
Paracá, Timbo or Oreja de Negro *(Enterolobilum timbouva)* fruits
Sacatrapo or Retortón *(Prosopis strombulifera)* fruits and roots
Araucanian Pangui *(Gunnea scabra, Urtica sp)* roots
Huique *(Coriana ruscifolia Feuillée)* branches
Maqui *(Aristotelia chilensis)*, blended with leaves of Concho de Molejón
Cochayuyo *(Durvilea antarctica)*
Itin *(Prosopis kuntzei)* crushed bark with with Mistol rind
Soot boiled for several hours
Walnut of the North *(Juglans australis)*
Black Voqui *(Muehlenbeckia hastulata)* bark

Churqui (Acacia cavenia)

Huique

Voqui Negro (Muehlenbeckia hastulata)

Looms

To define a loom it is necessary to describe the way weaving is performed in a loom. Weaving is just the recurrent interlacing of warp threads crossed by weft threads. The loom is the frame that helps maintain the position and spacing of the warp threads separated into two planes to form a shed for the shuttle to weave.

Both planes have an equal number of warp threads since they are formed by one of a pair, one of the planes will have heddles attached to them, which are auxiliary cords to tie the threads in order to ease the crossing in a rhythmic and mechanical form without having to cross each thread.

The native looms have heddles moved by hand. If the warp is too wide the heddles are tied to a reed to move them with only one movement.

The criollo looms are a copy of hose brought by the Spaniards and have another type of heddles, moved by treadles or hanging handles.

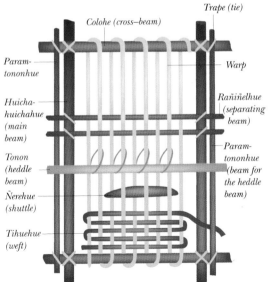

Trape (tie)

Colohe (cross–beam)

Param-tononhue

Warp

Huicha-huichahue (main beam)

Rañiñelhue (separating beam)

Tonon (heddle beam)

Param-tononhue (beam for the heddle beam)

Ñerehue (shuttle)

Tihuehue (weft)

Huitral, (Mapuche loom)

Aboriginal looms

Mapuche loom

Small back–strap loom

Loom used in the Puna

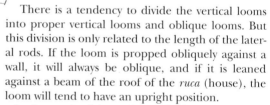

Back–strap loom

There are several types of native looms that aboriginals from South America have bequeathed us. They can be divided into two big groups: vertical and horizontal looms.

The vertical loom, used in the north of Argentina (Chaco and Catamarca) and in Alto Peru (Tarabuco and Potolo), consist of a frame of two parallel lateral rods and two crossbeams called warp rods.

The looms used in the south of Argentina and Chile have two supplementary pieces to support the heddle stick (*tononhue*), called *param–tononhue* by the Indians.

There is a tendency to divide the vertical looms into proper vertical looms and oblique looms. But this division is only related to the length of the lateral rods. If the loom is propped obliquely against a wall, it will always be oblique, and if it is leaned against a beam of the roof of the *ruca* (house), the loom will tend to have an upright position.

In the south of Argentina and Chile, Indians use looms that are leaned against a pair of wooden posts or forked props. The difference between these looms and the horizontal ones is not relevant since the different forms of looms do not change the weaving technique.

There is still another type of vertical loom called "Pampa–sash loom" or "small board loom" It is made up of two vertical posts staked into the ground, separated by the length of the piece to be weaved. The warp is not vertical but transverse; it usually has only one heddle and several small boards to keep the crossing in place and to tie the threads that have been chosen for the design.

The most common native horizontal loom is formed by four posts firmly staked into the ground forming the vertices of a rectangle. The two lateral rods are stuck in order to tense the warp threads, which is near the ground. The heddles rest directly on the warp. Another type of loom has two forked props to support the heddle stick.

Since the posts are firm, the weavers have to roll up the warp assembly and take it into their *rancho* (hut) during the night and then unwrap it again the next morning.

Sometimes the weaver sits on the already woven part, occasionally she rolls the cloth on a cross beam called the *"envolvedor"* (roller). In that case she ties the higher beam to the posts with a thick woollen rope and the rope will be untied while the weaver is finishing her piece.

The back–strap looms are also considered horizontal looms. One end of the loom is fastened to a tree or a post and the other end is tied around the waist of the weaver.

The maximum width that can be woven with horizontal looms is the distance the arms of the weaver can reach, around 0,85 m.

Another very picturesque loom is the "big toe loom". In this loom the warp threads are directly fastened to the big toe of the weaver, and the other end to the waist or neck. This is how sashes, garters, etc were woven, using the technique of a flat plait. The same name is given to the loom that has a stick in one end and is fastened between two toes.

Mapuche loom

Mapuche loom

Small boards loom

Looms of European Origin

Criollo loom used in Argentina, Peru and Bolivia to weave any type of cloth.

The *criollo* loom is a copy of the loom brought to America by Europeans and its use spread in the Northwest from the Puna to Cuyo. It is still used by the weavers in these provinces. It consists of four posts or forked props that hold two beams, where the rods are placed. This is necessary to hold the heddle–rope, which is moved by treadles and handles. Sometimes these looms have additional beams to hang the comb–reed with which the weft rows are packed taut.

The rollers are fixed with ties similar to those used in the yoke, at the height required by the weaver. As the cloth is woven, the warp–roller is unwrapped and the roller next to the weaver wraps up the finished cloth.

The *criollo* loom and the European loom were used in all Jesuitical textile workshops.

Juan León Pallière, (1823–1887) "Criollo loom"

In the north and centre of Argentina as well as in Cuyo, Bolivia, Peru and the northern region of Chile, horizontal, vertical and *criollo* looms were used, but in the northwest, they only wove in *criollo* looms. In Bolivia and Peru horizontal back–strap looms and the four posts ones were preferred. In the south only the vertical loom called *huitral* was and still is used today.

Small loom to weave rugs

Other Looms

There is a native invention, called by Fausto Burgos "small loom to weave plush carpets" which is nothing but a horizontal frame with a base of broad beams. The warp–assembly is round, so that it placed a-rounds the wood as if it were an endless skein. While weaving, the cloth hangs down, and when the piece is finished the warp threads that have not been woven are cut by half and left as a tasselled fringe.

Tassels made with a tassel loom

There are native and European tassel–looms. The native loom is vertical, with two posts, completed with one heddle and a small board so that the weft is left hanging loose at one of the borders to serve as tassel; whereas the European loom has a heddle reed, a device with separate openings and a central hole spaced at even distances, through which the successive warp threads are threaded to keep them parallel and properly spaced. The threads of one of the planes are threaded through the holes, and the threads of the other plane pass the openings. As the reed is moved up and down, the shed is opened for the weft to pass. The tassels are formed with the help of the small board.

warp

weft

braid   tassel

Tassel loom

Auxiliary tools

The weavers use auxiliary tools to complete their fabrics.

In the north, Quechuas and Aymaras used bone utensils to help themselves with the very thin threads they use in weft–face cloth.

Their names are *rockey*, a cuneiform tip (*huihuina* in the Puna), *huichuna* a sort of fork made from a bone of a vicuña foot and *mathina* a small board with a jagged border.

For warp–face cloth, they use a shuttle made of wood or bone that they called *kallhua* (*huinaza* in the Puna in Jujuy).

The Mapuche, Tehuelche and Pampa Indians (warp–face cloth weavers) always had this shuttle as an irreplaceable auxiliary element near the loom and they called it "*ñerehué*".

When they had to weave ponchos or any other piece which did not have the four borders, these shuttles were between 8 to 10 cm wide, and fairly long. If the piece had borders, then the shuttles had to be thinner, sometimes as thin as a pencil when the weaver got to the border and there were only some centimetres left, to pass the shuttle.

Wide and narrow shuttles

Huihuina

*C. E. Pellegrini
(1800–1875)
"Indians working"*

Rockey   *Huichuna*   *Mathina*

Weaving Techniques

Warp

The warp is the group of threads stretched lengthwise on the frame of a loom; they have to keep a certain tension and are wrapped in pairs so that the warp assembly can be divided in planes.

The weft is the weaving thread used crosswise of the warp through the sheds made by the heddles.

The different characteristics of the fabric will depend on the form the arrangement of these threads has been made.

Weft face

Weft Face Cloth

This is the name given to the type of hand–woven fabric in which only the weft shows, the warp threads are set so wide apart that the weft packs down between them and completely covers the warp.

This technique allows a design variation only limited by the weavers' imagination. Good examples for items woven with this technique are wall–hangings.

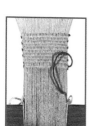

Warp face (white warp, red weft)

Warp Face Cloth

This is the name given to the type of hand woven fabric in which only the warp shows, and the weft remains hidden. The warp threads are set so closely together that the weft is entirely covered by them. Here the colour variation depends on the threads that were chosen when warping, and the designs will depend on this choice.

Balanced Cloth

This is the name given to the cloth in which both the warp and the weft can be seen. The technique was introduced by the conquerors and it can be seen in *barraganes, cordellates* and *picotes,* different names used to identify this type of cloth, which only differ in their design.

In many ponchos and fine vicuña blankets, woven in a *criollo* loom, we also find this balanced type of weaving. The tautness is done with a comb–reed that leaves light between the warp pairs, leaving to be seen all the threads that make up the fabric.

Balanced cloth (white warp, red weft)

Plain Weaving
This is the simplest weaving technique; many authors call it "poncho stitch" although the name seems to refer to nee-dle–work that is not the case. The cloth is formed by the interlacing of two sets of threads placed at right angles and in which the threads pass under and over one another in simple alternation. This technique allows the design of ikat.

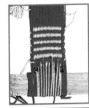

Peinecillo or Peinecilla (Small comb)
This technique includes a warping variant which con-sists of using threads of different colours for each of the two threads that make up the pair. From there on, in each crossing, the heddles bring up one of the two colours, producing an alternation that resem-bles the teeth of a comb.

It is still plain weaving but with special characteris-tics, if certain threads are lifted and others are pulled down, the design can be varied.

Small comb technique, both sides (white and red warp, white weft)

With the Mapuche supplementary tech-nique matras, saddle–bags, sashes and garters for boots are made.

Supplementary Warp Patterning
In this technique two or more colours of supple-mentary (additional) threads lie between the foun-dation warp and are lifted to the surface to create the design.

If in a fabric woven with this system, the threads

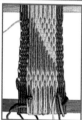

Suplementary warp cloth, both sides, false double face

Complementary warp technique

Double face

False double face

that carry the design are taken away, the piece will not loose its structure, but it will have a peculiar feature, the warp threads do not cross one by one, as is plain weaving, but two by two.

In this structure the warp pairs are composed of three threads, although the elements of the pair continue being two: the colourful design thread and the natural thread formed by two threads put parallel to the sides of the former.

In the Mapuche culture, this technique is used to weave *matras*, *cutamas*, and belts, it is also found in *trarilonkos* (headwear) and garters for the boots (called "*ataderas*" in Cuyo) and in some ponchos.

Complementary Warp Patterning

In this structure, the complementary warp assembly will not only carry the design but it will also form part of the structure of the fabric.

The cloth will be thicker because the threads are organized into two layers. A longitudinal cut of the cloth would show four threads, one on top of the other, instead of two, which are found in plain weaving.

This technique needs double pairs of warp threads. In Argentina there are two types of fabrics that are woven with this warping system, the so called "*laboreo*" system (pattern band) with double warp and simple weft, used in the ornamentation of ponchos, sashes, rugs (*lamas* in Mapuche language) and saddlebags (*alforjas*) and the flat tubular system, or double cloth used exclusively for the weaving of belts.

Double Faced and False Double Faced Textiles

The double–faced fabrics are reversible, with the same designs appearing in opposite (positive/negative and negative/positive) colour combinations on each side. The items woven with complementary warp — *laboreo* (pattern band) and tubular — belong to this category. For a fabric to be double-faced it has to fulfil the following condition: each thread that carries a design on one side must have the corresponding colour on the other.

The fabrics with supplementary warp patterning are classified as "of false double face" because they do not fulfil the condition mentioned above, although it might look as if they did. The threads do not have a pair that will replace them on the opposite side, there is just an absence of thread which allows the weft to be seen.

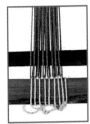

Four-border technique, way of tying the warp

Four Borders Cloth

In all pre-Hispanic cultures the weavers produced finished garments, they did not weave just plain cloth. It was a European idea, to weave cloth and then make garments out of it.

A *criollo* poncho will invariably have hems at both ends, whereas the others made by Indians have tassels from the warp or they have the four borders.

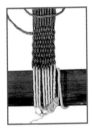

The weft is started at the border against the frame

For the four-border cloth, the weaver has to begin to tie the warp from the border of the frame, leaving the frame outside the warp. So, the pairs of warp have to be tied to the frame one by one.

The weaving is started from both sides at the same time, finishing the cloth somewhere in the middle. The weaver has to change her tools when the unwoven space begins to diminish and she has to finish her work with a needle.

End of a four-border cloth

Warp Fringes and All–round Tassels

Ponchos and belts have fringes as a finishing. The garments used by the Mapuche Indians usually have warp tassels that appear in both ends of the cloth, they are also called structural tassels because they are the threads of the warp.

Warp or structural tassel

In the trariwes, the belts used by the Mapuche women, we find the 30–cm–long tassels plaited or tied in two groups forming an important part of the ornamentation.

In Inca textiles — Quechua and Aymaras — the ponchos have all–round tassels. These tassels contained in a braid or stripe, usually woven apart, are formed by the crossing that surpasses the width of the stripe. That braid is sewn around the poncho as an ornament. They are made of very colourful wool and are not longer than three or four centimetres.

Tasselled fringe sewn around the four borders

In the *criollo* ponchos, the tassels, which are a bit longer, are also sewn, as it was done with the Inca ponchos but they are usually monochrome: the predominant colour of the garment.

The way these bands of fringe are made has already been explained in the chapter about different types of looms.

There are other types of tassels, which have been found in archaeological sites but are no longer produced. They are called "*flecos de cinta*" (ribbon tassels). They are made at the beginning and ending of a piece of cloth and are woven with several threads taken from the warp, each with several threads taken together. A separate piece is then produced. The weaver may leave these multiple threads and continue with only one all around the warp, originating only one piece of cloth.

Tasselled fringe sewn on hem

Warp–Ikat Patterning

This ornamentation is made while dying. When the weaver decides on the design, she will start tying different groups of warp threads so that the dye will not penetrate the tied parts. The Mapuche Indians call it *trarikán* and the *Quechua, watai* (in both cases the words mean tied)

After making all necessary ties, the warp is removed from the loom, taking the precaution to use a rope (tying all ends with a loose knot in order not to harm the parts to be dyed) to pass along the place that the warp–beams had taken, keeping things in the right place in order not to have unnecessary problems when putting the warp back into place once the process of dying is finished.

This technique is used to make ponchos, blankets and carpets. In the Mapuche culture, the ponchos ornamented with this technique were only for the *Cacique* (chief). They were called *Trarikanmakuñ* (*trarin*: to tie; *makuñ*: poncho).

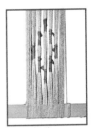

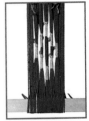

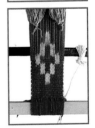

Warp–ikat technique, tying, dyeing, untying and weaving

Ponchos

Poncho use in the world

- *South and Central America*
- *Leather poncho-style shirt area*
- *Eskimos*
- *Cedar bark poncho*
- *Tibet and Mongolia*
- *Borneo and Taiwan*
- *Micronesia*
- *Syria*
- *Germanic peoples*
- *Sierra Morena*
- *Canary Islands*
- *French Guiana, and Cameroon*
- *Laplanders*
- *Hunters of northern Rusia*

The etymology of the word "poncho" is uncertain. It can be described as a square piece of cloth with a slit in the middle through which the head is passed. It covers from the neck down to the legs, depending

on the height of the user. There are some ponchos from Chile or the Alto Peru, what today is Bolivia, which only reach the waist, whereas there are other types of ponchos, called *talares* (ankle–length) because they reach the ankles. The poncho has been used and is still used in rural areas in Argentina and all neighbouring countries.

In South America the use of the poncho spread all along the Andean region, reaching after the discovery of America, from Colombia to the Amazonas plain and to the Pampas in Argentina. The region where archaeological ponchos have been found is much smaller. Archeological ponchos have only been found to the south of the Atacama Puna and the

Pre–Columbian poncho

Juan Manuel Blanes (1830–1901) "Lonely gaucho"

coast of Peru. It is possible that the region might have been bigger in pre–historic times but there are no proofs so far.

The use of the poncho had spread down the Andean corridor, especially at the time when Tupac Inca, incorporated, in the sixteenth century, the north-western part of Argentina and Cuyo to the Tawan-tinsuyo and spread the textile culture the Incas had acquired from other, much older civilizations such as Tihuanaco. The proof of this is the mummy of An-gualasto found in the province of San Juan (Argen-tina) dated around 1200 AD to 1400 AD.

Detail of the slit of the poncho of the Angualasto mummy, Etnographic Museum Juan B. Ambrosetti, Buenos Aires

Although it has been proven that the poncho al-ready existed in pre–Christian times, this garment seems to have rapidly gained in importance after the arrival of the Spanish conquerors to America. Its use was spread by the missionaries for aesthetic reasons as well as for modesty, "to cover the nakedness" of the Indians, and by Spanish merchants who not only benefited with this trade, but when crossing the country with their loaded trunks, also helped spread uses and customs.

María Delia Millán de Palavecino, quoting Vidau-rre (Peruvian writer, 1772–1841), writes that it is believed that the introduction of the horse favoured the use of the poncho, because it allowed more com-fortable movements.

Angualasto mummy, Etnographic Museum Juan B. Ambrosetti, Buenos Aires

"The missionary work of the Catholic Church in the sixteenth and seventeenth centuries established the general use of garments, and an orderly system to obtain and prepare woollen textiles, was cre-ated. There was a tendency to pro-vide the Indians with standard clothes, which were made either of wool or the 'poor canvas of the earth'.

These garments were a distinguishing charac-teristic of the Indians who lived in the mis-sions because they copi-ed the Spanish clothes. They consisted of a pair of trousers, a jacket and a poncho.

That was the situation of the use of the aboriginal poncho among the Araucanos, the Patagonians and the Indians living in the Chaco in the seventeenth century.

The chronicles of the time explain that occasional-ly during the conquest, the Spaniards were some-times forced to adopt Indian clothes when they were not able to have their garments brought from Spain. The poncho became a comfortable substitute for the Spanish cloak."

We have to stress this last sentence, because it makes it clear that the poncho does not derive from the Spanish cloak. Little by little, the poncho became a substitute for the cloak, out of necessity and out of preference.

This new market and the influence of the mission-aries, especially the Jesuits, are the two features that started the trend to mix the designs used in textiles. The weavers used not only purely American motifs, but they included European designs as well. That is the reason why there are motifs from heraldic shields as the double–headed eagle of the House of Habsburg and the fleur–de–lis of the Bourbon era.

F. Paucke S. J. (1719–1779) "Llamas and guanacos"

Much has been writ-ten on this noble gar-ment, synonym of South America nowa-days. An idea of the universality of the poncho and its origin is given by María Delia Guillán de Palavecino. This tire-less Argentine con-temporary researcher has studied it with scientific rigor. Her field observations and research are pre-sented in her work "El Poncho".

F. Paucke S. J. (1719–1779) "San Javier celebration "

R. Ramos "Ceferino Namuncurá", 1993

R. Ramos "Towards Neuquén" 1991

The abbot Juan Ignacio Molina explained in his chronicle that "the wives of the *Cacique* (chief) were forced every year to give their husband apart from the necessary garments, another blanket called poncho which is one of the most important garments in the American trade".

This trade was immediately started by the Spanish merchants who made an annual tour to buy textiles in the native communities and which were then sold in the cities.

The Jesuit priest Florian Paucke, in the eighteenth century, described the gear of the Guarani Indians, he wrote: *"The clothes are made up of a pair of trousers, a bodice and a woven blanket approximately three yards long and two yards wide. This white cloth has a slit in the middle for the Indian to pass his head through. This blanket hangs from the shoulders and arms down to the ankles and it has tassels made of cotton on both sides. In winter these blankets are made of wool."*

As he travelled from Buenos Aires to the Andes, he wrote: *"They do not have downy blankets, but a woven rug is tightly fit around them. It reaches down to their knees. Another, bigger blanket coveres the upper part of the body and in the centre it has a hole through which they pass their head and leave the rug to hang down their bodies."*

It was Florian Paucke who introduced the poncho among the Mocobí Indians in Santa Fe, and he himself taught the Indians the process of spinning, dyeing and weaving. It was the first time the Mocobí Indians came into contact with the art of weaving.

F. Paucke S. J. (1719–1779) "Indian woman with a spear"

Paucke also refers to the trade with Paraguay, saying in a note that he had sent seventy–three finished blankets manufactured by the Indians for the first time. He received for them, forty eight *quintales* (1 *quintal* =100 lbs.) of Paraguayan herb and fifteen *quintales* of tobacco."

Juan Manuel Blanes, (1830–1901), untitled

The woven fabrics from the south were massively introduced during the Campaign to the Desert when General Julio Argentino Roca (1843–1914) conquered Patagonia. The small settlements along the frontier were constantly harassed by hostile Indian tribes who also attacked the Indians who lived peacefully and worked in the farms. Their women wove saddle–blankets and ponchos for the people in the farms.

After the Campaign, many Indians were taken prisoner and given to well–off families. María Leuvú wrote the way in which many of the prisoners were given to an Indian called Ramón Cabral, one of Roca's friend: *"The captives were taken to Buenos Aires and given to different families. Quintuillán (her mother) was given together with her grandmother, who was still young, and two other Indian women. In their new homes they were given wool to weave. They had to prepare a loom and started making ponchos and saddle blankets. Sometimes they were taken to a nearby square and since they did not know Spanish, they were accompanied by a black woman who lived with them."*

It was right after the south was pacified, that the use of the poncho began to spread, especially the poncho called *pampa* or poncho *de guarda atada* (warp–ikat poncho)

These ponchos carry the design of a cross or steps, which are made with the technique called ikat or *ikaten*.

The French naturalist Arsène Isabelle wrote about the poncho in 1830 and 1834:"It is a piece of wool and cotton or cotton and wool striped with different colours. It is seven hand–spans wide and twelve long with a slit in the centre to pass the head."

The ponchos with fringes or *calles de laboreo*, (pattern bands), coming from the provinces of the north, including the Alto Peru (even after its declaration of independence in 1825) were used until the second half of the nineteenth century.

Emeric Essex Vidal described in 1816 the ponchos used in the Province of Buenos Aires:

"The poncho is the outer garment worn by all the country people of these provinces. It is composed of two pieces of cloth, seven feet long and two wide, sewed together lengthwise, except in the middle, where sufficient room is left to put the head through. It is believed that throughout the province of Buenos Ayres there is not one creole manufactory of these articles, though they are in such general use. At Salta in Peru, which is famous for the manufacture of ponchos, they are made of cotton, of great beauty and high price; but those made by the humble Indians of the Pampas (plains) are of wool, so close and strong as to resist a very heavy rain, the patterns curious and original, the colours generally sober but lasting; though they have dyes of the most brilliant hues, which they apply to other purposes. By the Indians themselves the poncho is not much worn".

Emeric Essex Vidal (1791–1861) "Town hall" (detail)

Parts of the Poncho

llanca (reinforcement)

The slit for the head to pass through is called "mouth".

The bands are columns of different colours.

The background colour of a poncho is called field. The stripes are on the field.

The bands or columns are areas of supplementary and complementary warp with pattern–bands that decorate the item.

Warp–ikat bands are separated by background colours and by colour stripes. When the warp–ikat covers the whole poncho it is called a cross–coated poncho.

Pattern–band slit (Jesuitical poncho)

Excentric design slit (Pilagá poncho)

Striped slit with a box (poncho from Mendoza)

Craid slit (70 stripes poncho)

Ponchos from the North

As a general rule, we have to bear in mind that the ponchos from the north of Argentina and from the Alto Peru, are always woven in two halves and are sewn in the middle.

The loom is always horizontal, but in Argentina the *criollo* loom is also used, which is an adaptation of the Spanish loom, whereas in the Alto Peru the four post loom is preferred.

*Poncho
from Alto Peru*

The other difference is the technique. The Argentine weavers use a long warp which has twice the length of the poncho and weave the cloth lengthwise. Once they have finished it, they take it off the loom, cut it in half, put both sides one in front of the other and sew it together, leaving an opening for the "mouth". Then they sew the hem for a better finishing and put a tasselled fringe all around the poncho, which they have woven in the small loom called "tassel loom".

*Poncho
from Alto Peru*

In the Bolivian Altiplano, each half is woven separately, as if it were just one piece with four borders. The second half will be a copy of the first one, that is the reason why, due to their simple technique, the second will never be exactly alike, and as they usually have a tasselled fringe all around, the piece keeps its aesthetic value.

The best ponchos from the north come from Catamarca, although all the provinces in that area have had and still have, an excellent textile production.

Peruvian poncho

The ponchos from the north have stripes, the traditional ones from Salta, for example, are red and purple with a black band, but there are also ponchos

Vicuña poncho
from Alto Peru

Poncho
from Catamarca

Poncho from
Santiago del Estero

B. Franklin Rawson
(1819–1871)
"Broom seller"

in which the ikat technique has been used or the ponchos with rings dyed with the plangit technique.

The ponchos from Alto Peru have an important ornamentation and a great variety of designs. Many of them are made with alpaca wool.

Stripes, ikat, (*huatay* or *huatado*), double–faced pattern bands (*pallai*), can be seen in the same piece, depending on the ornamentation used in the region it has been woven. Some have a tasselled fringe, some a pattern band, still others, the most important ones, band and tassels; others have neither fringes nor bands.

Poncho from Salta

The ponchos and blankets made of vicuña wool from Belén in the province of Catamarca have mythical fame because of the delicacy and fineness with which they have been woven. These women are the heirs of the weavers of *cumbi*, the high quality fabrics woven for the Inca. The ponchos are generally woven in two matching oblong halves and are then sewn together, whereas the blankets are woven in just one piece. Both have hems and a tasselled fringe.

The most important ornament of these ponchos is its embroidered design performed with the same yarn.

Poncho from Jujuy

In Bolivia the vicuña ponchos are heavier, with four borders, always woven in two halves and are very rarely embroidered. Sometimes the ponchos were woven matching a shawl.

Silk ponchos have also been woven in the looms in the northwest, but they are rare. Sometimes there are ponchos with mixed silk and vicuña wool, sometimes even with sheep's wool or with cotton.

Poncho from Salta

Ponchos from the South

Mapuche loom

The first known ponchos from the south were made of guanaco or skunk leather, which the Indians kneaded and rubbed vigorously with raw, previously chewed liver. Then they were sewn with fine threads made of tendons and to hide the seams, they stretched and painted them carefully, usually with red and black geometric patterns.

The gauchos also wore leather ponchos, but they were made with well–kneaded horse skin. They were seamless had rounded edges and resembled a Spanish cloak.

After the leather poncho, the woollen poncho started being used, woven in vertical looms. At the very beginning, guanaco wool was used, after the Conquest, sheep's wool was preferred.

Emile Lassalle (1813–1871) "Patagons"

Pampa ponchos or technically "ponchos *de guarda atada*" (warp–ikat pattern ponchos), are very beautiful, as the ponchos with pattern bands, the double faced ones (with complementary warp) or the false double faced pampa ponchos (with supplementary warp), are beautiful.

Striped poncho

The latter are called Mapuche, which is the name given to the Indians who lived in the south of Argentina (Araucano is the name given to the Mapuche Indians who lived in the south of Chile).

The warp–ikat pattern ponchos are usually black, blue–black or burgundy coloured and their designs are generally crosses, rhombuses or steps, woven in natural wool.

The ponchos with pattern bands or plain bands can also be black, white and burgundy coloured.

Sobremakuň

In the south, the ponchos are woven in vertical looms in only one piece, taking special care at the height of the thirty or thirty–five centimetres slit and weaving it with non continuous wefts. Both ends of the "mouth" have a reinforcement called *llanca*. The big difference with the ponchos from the north are the tassels, in the south they are a continuation of the warp (warp tassels or structural tassels), that is to say there are tassels only in both extremes and they form part of the weaving. In the ponchos from the north, the tassels are sewed all around the borders.

Poncho with stripes

The ideal poncho is 180 cm long and 140 cm wide, but there are very old ponchos, which are much smaller. The Mapuche word for poncho is *makuň*, which is the name given to the simple items, those which have no ornaments and with only one band.

The *wirikan–makuň* (*wirin*=band) is the striped poncho, it is formed by bands of several colours which are repeated in an established order. The most beautiful ones are dark red, golden yellow and dark blue, but other colours are also used and they are always very well combined. The Mapuche Indians even use different shades of brown or dark brown in their ponchos.

Poncho with stripes

The ponchos without fringes are very valuable because they have been woven with the four borders technique.

The *ñimin–makuñ* (*ñimin* = design obtained by weaving) is the poncho with pattern bands, also called Andean or Araucanian technique and it produces double faced designs also used for the Araucanian sash, called *trarihue*.

Checked poncho

These items have a more or less complicated ornamentation, they have two or more bands or they are woven with several bands as ponchos with chequer board designs.

The most difficult part of this technique is the difference in rhythm when weaving.

The technique for the Pampa ponchos is Araucanian, it came with the Mapuche Indians across the Andes, and they probably learnt it from the Indians that came from the north, maybe the Incas.

The ponchos called *trarikan–makuñ* (*trarin*=tied) or poncho *de guarda atada* (tied pattern poncho), have been woven with the famous resist dye technique, internationally known as ikat. The weavers spend several weeks preparing the design before starting with the weaving.

The warp is formed with natural wool, then 4 to 6 cm of some threads of the warp (from 10 to 20) are covered with loamy white earth called *mallo–mallo* and tied with vegetable fibres or wool.

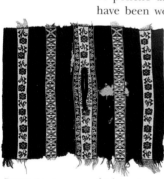

Pattern–band poncho

It is difficult to explain, but to design steps, crosses and rhombuses is even more complicated. The preparing of 400 to 1600 ties is an art for experts. Then the warp is taken off the loom for dyeing. After soaking it in the dye bath, the warp is placed again in the loom, some of the ties are loosened and weaving can be started. The ties are loosened when the weaving progresses, because if all warp threads are loosened before starting, they will move and the result would be a blurred design.

Once all these previous steps have been taken care of, mechanical weaving can begin.

The tassels of these ponchos are warp tassels, also called structure tassels.

Different ornamental designs can be found in the same piece. It is a *trarikan––ñimin–makuñ* if the warp–ikat patterning and the pattern bands have been used, a *wirikan–ñimin–makuñ* if it has stripes and pattern bands, a *wirikan–külatrarin–makuñ* if it has stripes and warp–*ikat* patterning and a *wirikan–ñimin–külatrarin–makuñ* if it has stripes, pattern bands and three warp–ikat patterning bands.

Warp–ikat and pattern–band poncho

Items of exceptional beauty are the *sobremakuñ*. They are small ponchos, woven with rich pattern bands that have a wide fringe band all around the borders (*wincha*) which has a ceremonial function. For the poncho *de argollas* (poncho with rings) a different method of resist dyeing is used.

Striped warp–ikat poncho

Warp–ikat poncho

The technique is called *plangit* or *plangi*.

The poncho is woven with natural wool and then parts of the cloth are tied around small stones, only then, the poncho is soaked in the dye bath.

G. Milet Ramírez (1860–1917) "Lloncon chief"

When the stones are untied, the poncho is ornamented with shapes in the form of rings.

Square figures or rhombuses can also be achieved if the cloth is folded and then tied.

These ponchos are usually made of finer wool because the tying requires a more flexible cloth and because it is not easy to dye dark and even colours using a thicker fabric. There were ponchos with rings with and without tassels. The weavers had learnt these techniques from Indians coming from the north, along the Andean corridor, because they are similar to the techniques used in those regions.

Striped warp–ikat poncho

Poncho with rings

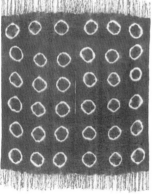

Using these basic techniques, the Indian weavers used their imagination to combine bands, warp–ikat patterning and pattern bands to produce extraordinary items. And the finished work had its compensations. Accomplished weavers were respected members of the community and the chief could be proud of his wives.

We cannot say that the complexity of a piece, the colours of the stripes, the existence of pattern bands had an established meaning in its owner's political or military hierarchy, but from what we have just explained, we can infer that

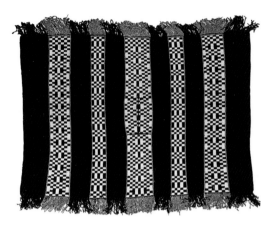

Pattern–band poncho

the more important the position a man had, the better weavers he would have and thus have better ponchos.

Today there are many weavers, but there are very few who devote themselves to the weaving of these traditional pampa ponchos. It is much easier to produce smaller items or sashes with tassels as decoration items or souvenirs; apart from that, the huge looms, which can be three by two metres, are not easy to handle. Yet there are still some weavers, which make excellent ponchos, using all the techniques described in this chapter.

The only difference between these ponchos and the old ones is that they lack that typical matt shine (similar to that of acrylic fibres) of the wool of the sheep that were found in the south two centuries ago.

Striped pattern–band poncho

Jesuitical Ponchos

At the time of the Inca Empire, the textile production was considerable, but it was not enough to cover the needs of the new society formed after the conquest. The items were woven one by one and its quality and form were not adapted to the system used in Europe. There, the garments were cut and sewn from long pieces of fabric.

F. Paucke, S. J. (1719–1779) "Garments"

One of the alternatives to solve the problem was the importation of cloth from Europe or the creation of textile centres that would make cloth the way it was made in Europe. The second solution was adopted. Luxury fabrics such as cashmere cloth came from England, lace from Flanders, satins and brocades from Italy and woollen cloth from Castile, but the most important part of the fabrics used was manufactured in America.

The first textile workshop established by the Company of Jesus was from 1545, only five decades after the arrival of Columbus to America.

The site chosen by the Jesuits was the town of Sapallanga, located in the valley of Jauja, in Peru, and from there they were spread all over America, until the Jesuits were expelled in the year 1767.

The need to have these fabrics, grew and became really important for the residents of the New World, especially because of the laws passed by the Cortes in Valladolid. In 1548, for example, the laws forbade the colonies to buy cloth in Spain, because it was thought that the demand would increase the prices in the Iberian Peninsula.

A year later, the opposite law was passed, it forbade the manufacture of fine cloth in America, and in 1552, to continue with this erratic policy, the Crown forbade the exportation of woollen cloth or "anything made of wool".

The best quality ponchos were manufactured in Peru and in Alto Peru, although the best organization of the Company of Jesus was in Paraguay, were they had created the Jesuitical Province called *Paracuaria*.

In Argentina the most important centres of poncho production were Tucumán, Córdoba and Catamarca. While in the first two, the ponchos were woven with sheep's wool, in Catamarca they took advantage of the cotton that was massively produced in the region.

In these workshops, the looms were of the Spanish style, with treadles, with which they could weave items up to a yard of width by 120 yards long. They used any type of yarn, cotton, sheep's wool, alpaca (only in Alto Peru) and mixed fibres.

The ponchos were manufactured, weaving long items of a width of between 20 and 30 cm. They formed each half sewing lengthwise three bands cut from the original cloth, which were then placed symmetrically as if in a mirror.

They were usually sewn leaving the central part open, or the central band was woven with the slit with discontinuous weft.

F. Paucke S. J.
(1719–1779)
"Indian weaving"

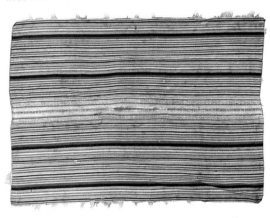

Jesuitical poncho

The quality and variety of designs are very important, there are simple ponchos made of striped cloth, there are ponchos with striped sides and with the central band woven with a double faced pattern band, and the best ones are those woven only with the pattern band technique, always repeating the same design sequence.

They always had a hem at both ends and a tasselled fringe was sewn all around the poncho. This way of finishing the poncho greatly influenced the textiles in the northwest of Argentina.

Although after 1767, many workshops were abandoned, others, especially those located in the Andean region, went on with their work, until it came to a halt in 1781 with the Indian uprising of Amaru and Katari.

Jesuitical poncho

Other Ponchos

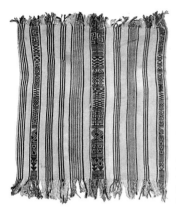

Pilagá poncho

Seventy–stripes poncho woven in one piece. It has a pattern–band braid all around and around the slit and a tasseled fringe with fine threads.

Adolphe D'Hastrel (1805–1875) "Lancer"

The natives of the region of the Chaco, a region that covers the territory of various Argentine provinces as Santa Fe, Chaco, Formosa, Santiago del Estero and Salta, and parts of the neighbouring countries of Paraguay and Bolivia, have devoted themselves to the weaving of cotton fibres, wool and a vegetable called *caraguatá*. With this fibre obtained from the ground leaves of a plant, spun by rubbing these leaves between the hand and the thigh and coloured with vegetable dyes, they wove a great variety of items such as bags, sashes and shirts.

The most important ponchos are called *pilagá*, the name of the Indian tribe who weave it. Usually they are made of sheep's wool, woven in a vertical loom similar to the loom used by the Mapuches, in only one piece, with warp or structural tassels, and only occasionally finished with a hem and a tasselled fringe.

They have faded colours obtained by dyeing the ponchos with vegetable dyes. Its ornamentation consists of pattern bands combined with other techniques such as supplementary warp or false double face technique, complementary warp (Andean double face or pattern bands) and designs with the "small comb technique". The lack of symmetry is another important feature of these ponchos.

There are also ponchos with rings obtained by the plangit technique made by the Guaycurú Indians, but the traditional ones are those with pattern bands.

The ponchos called "of seventy stripes" are made in Paraguay and are used in the province of Corrientes. They are made of cotton and occasionally silk, with thin stripes of white and another colour such as brown, blue, grey, red or black. Woven in one piece, they have a pattern band fringe with tassels all around the poncho and around the slit.

As it has been said before, this book will just describe textiles woven in Argentina, but we cannot fail to mention the English ponchos that had had their origin in the industrial revolution, that forced Great Britain to sell their production surplus.

English poncho (obverse)

Especially from 1765 on, when steam started being applied to the textile industry and the speed of cloth producing machines was considerably increased. The English had learnt from many travellers that the poncho was widely used in South America so they started manufacturing them.

The quality and the designs of the ponchos brought from England greatly varied, the most common ones were made of balanced cloth (showing warp and weft, the warp was usually made of cotton and the weft was made of wool). They produced some, which resembled the common striped rough texture poncho of the south and others with the designs of the Pampa ponchos made of fulled pure wool cloth. Some were even designed with ornaments that did not have any relation to the native ponchos.

English poncho (reverse)

These ponchos had sometimes leopard skin designs or Asian ornaments of columns encircled by snakes, designs, which were in fashion in London at that time.

The fabrics were manufactured in pieces of 140 cm wide and hundreds of metres long. The ponchos were then cut from those pieces and the borders

Poncho patrio

This dark blue garment with red lining is actually a sort of cloak–poncho with neck and front and rounded edges similar to those used in Castilla in the south of Chile and military uniforms. A company produced them in Montevideo (Uruguay).

were fringed with a band of velvet or wool. The tassels were made by twisting and gluing warp threads. But there were also ponchos with all around tassels: warp and weft tassels.

From the first half of the nineteenth century to the beginnings of the twentieth century, the textile industry in Birmingham and Manchester produced ponchos to be exported to the Río de la Plata, and according to Taullard, they were received by stores like Barclay, Campbell & Co and the store of the Ackerley brothers.

It is said, and it is probably true, that the complete piece of cloth was sometimes sent from England, and the ponchos were then finished in Buenos Aires.

The cloth used to manufacture the uniforms of the Argentine and Uruguayan army and police called poncho *patrio*, was also imported from Europe.

Juan Manuel Blanes
(1830–1901)
"Two Ponchos"
"Sentry"

Crosses, Steps and Rhombuses

In Machu Pichu the same symbolism is expressed in the tomb or royal mausoleum where there are four steps that do not have any function.

The ponchos made with the warp–ikat or pattern band techniques show stepped designs. They look like rhombuses one on top of the other or framed crosses.

There are a lot of studies about this design and some of them have arrived to completely dissimilar conclusions.

An important opinion is that of the Chilean scientist, Pedro Mege Rosso, who says that when a *trarikan–makun* is observed, it has to be interpreted as lines that cross the field of a poncho in a longitudinal axis, that is to say, following the threads of the warp, with a serpentine, staggered or undulating line. It is the *wirin* (line) design, born from the *praprawe* (labyrinth), duplicated and unfolded after suffering various changes that vary its initial form. According to the Mapuche cosmo vision, this *praprawe* leads to the stepped *wiring*, and using those steps, the *machi* ascended to the spiritual world.

Chakana in Tihuanaco

In the 30s, the Argentine architect Héctor Greslebin, wrote: "All the peoples who weave, fall into the same decorative and geometrical expressions. That is the reason why it is very difficult, almost impossible, to assert something about its origin, bearing in mind the comparison and identification of the same motifs. As for their origin, we cannot compare these geometrical forms, derived from weaving, with those that, although identical, derive from simplification of realistic themes and thus acquire symbolic expressions after having undergone stylisation processes, expressing abstract, totemic or religious ideas."

The differences between both researchers is notable, what for Mege Rosso is symbolism, for Greslebin is an act of geometrical design.

But there is a third point of view. When visiting the Altiplano, one is continually confronted with these stepped structures. To begin with, the famous cultivation platforms repeat the steps. They also form part of their constructions and monuments for their gods.

There is a close similarity between the crosses of the south and those found in Ollantaytambo. In the Sun Temple there are again four steps, which resemble the warp–ikat crosses of the Mapuche ponchos.

The oldest representations are those that can be seen in Tihuanaco in a construction called *Kantatallita*. Various stone blocks called *chakanas* are found there. There are two types of chakanas, square ones (with crosses in two levels) and with the form of rhombuses (crosses in four levels) which are supposed to have been constructed during the Empire.

In the monuments and constructions of the Inca period, we also find the crosses and the steps, probably due to Tihuanaco influence.

How did these symbols become a part of the cultural characteristics of the Mapuche Indians, if the Inca conquerors never crossed the river Maule, and the Araucanian dominions were further south? The Spanish only came into contact with them but in their military campaigns and never got further than the river Bio–Bio.

We do not know how, but we cannot dismiss the theory of the incorporation of these forms into the Mapuche textile culture, even when we cannot explain why they are used as a Mapuche ornamental design.

Mapuche warp–ikat poncho. The field is covered with crosses.

Matra

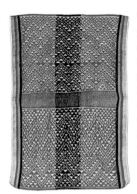

The *matra* was a fundamental piece of the gaucho's saddle and was an element that he adopted from the Indians. The function of the *matra* is exactly the same as the function of the *mandil*. It is a saddle cloth that not only protects the back of the horse from possible injuries that the saddle might produce, but it was also the gaucho's bed when he had to sleep in the open air.

The *matra* is of Araucanian origin made of sheep's wool, woven in a vertical loom. This saddle blanket is warp faced, has four borders and ornamental designs.

There are three ornamental techniques that may be found in a *matra*: *peinecillo* (small comb), geometric designs made with the technique of false double face and supplementary warp and bands of plain weave in different colours. The three techniques can be found in the same piece and are symmetrically arranged.

They have a rectangular form, although they may have a narrowing in the middle of the warp assembly, which gives them the form of a sandglass.

There are very big *matras*, called *matrones*, which have the size of a travel blanket, although the ones woven in the twentieth century are from 1 to 1,25 m long and between 0,90 and 1,10 m wide.

Mapuche matras

Criollo saddle with matras

The older items are not so wide but have more or less the same length.

Justo P. Sáenz explains that *"the big matra, of Araucanian origin of simple domestic manufacture, was an important part of the gaucho's bed. Today it has been replaced by a piece of felt called mandil".*

Bottom blanket

In his glossary he writes: *"matra also called jerga, a woollen or cotton–made thick and rough blanket, which conveniently folded on the back of the horse, has the same function as the mandil. They may have different origins, Pampa matras, made by Pampa Indians, which are the most famous ones because of the quality of their weaving and beauty of their colours. They are still used as blankets or soft mattresses to sleep on the ground. That is the origin of the expression gaucho matrero, the gaucho who lived away from civilization, in conflict with the law, and who was forced to sleep on his matra."*

First matra

Second matra

The colours of the *matras* are varied, at the beginning they were dyed with natural dye–stuff, generally with vegetable substances, today anilines may be used. They were dyed in bright and attractive colours and the soft and attenuated colours they show today are due to the passing of time, the light of the sun, the saline sweat of the horse and the constant rubbing of the fibre. There are some which just have the natural colour of the wool without dye; others have designs in darker colours which are "painted" with threads of the supplementary warp.

Third matra

The designs are always geometrical, without exception, although the designs can be the representation of stars (rhombuses), trees (repeated triangles), farm elements (hooks), guanaco eyes (rhombuses), ñandu anus (rhombus), wooden stirrups (double line triangles), spiders (hooked rhombuses), hills and rivers (simple or double lines in zigzag that cross the whole cloth) etc.

Leather carona

Bastos

The rhombus is a recurrent theme influenced by the oblique sense of the drawing forced by the weaving technique.

These rhombuses have been interpreted by researchers as the representation of the cardinal points, of great importance in the Mapuche culture. These Indians divided space into North and West as places with a negative connotation and South and East with a positive connotation.

Boleadoras

Stirrups

Girth and encimera

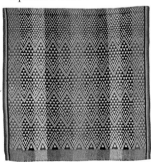

The East had for the Mapuche Indians a beneficial effect because it was related to the place where the sun rises.

This is emphasized by a habit they had, when a baby was born, the mother had to give birth facing the East.

Cojinillo

Complete saddle

Ristro

The *ristro* is the name given to the big *matra* used in Mendoza. It is one of the saddle blankets and it is used on the back of the horse folded in four. The *ristro* is of Mapuche origin, and the word *ristro* derives from the Mapuche word "*richro*" which means straight.

Ristro

Jergón

When the French explorer and naturalist Alcide D'Orbigny described the criollo saddle as the saw it in 1826 and 1833 he wrote: "...one or two blankets (jerga) the finer of which goes on top."

If the *ristro* comes from the south, the *jergón* is a *matra* that was used in the northwest. They are woven it two pieces sewn in the middle. They have a colourful ornamentation, made with the warp–ikat technique and they are finished with a hem at both ends.

If the influence comes from Alto Peru, they may have four borders. They have the size of a blanket.

Pelero

The *pelero* is the woven cloth that is put next to the back of the horse. It has to be thick, padded and absorbent of the sweat of the horse and they have to take the form of the horse to protect it from the injuries that the saddle might produce. The *pelero* has replaced the bare, kneaded sheepskin which was used as *"bajera"* (bottom blanket) from the beginning of equestrian use in South America.

The technique used to weave a pelero and a caronilla is very simple and resembles the technique used to make baskets.

The *pelero* is used in the whole country nowadays, but its origin and production centres are in the provinces of Cuyo, to the northwest of the Pampas and especially in Santiago del Estero.

It is a piece woven in what is called *"semitelar"*, a "semi–loom" which is a frame where the warp without the heddles is placed. The weft is crossed with two threads of wool, interwoven in each crossing. The result is a weft faced rug, two centimetres thick and 50 to 60 cm wide by 70 to 80 cm long.

The yarn is thick and loosely twisted, usually of only one thread and as thick as the little finger. The designs are geometrical, in zigzags or spotted, in two contrasting natural colours, the most common ones being brown and white.

Emeric Essex Vidal (1791–1861) "Gaucho with eighteenth century garment" and "Foreman"

Caronillas

Although the *caronilla* is sometimes called *pelero*, a *caronilla* is somewhat different. The wool is thick, but finely spun and twisted with two threads. It is bigger than the *pelero* and has colourful geometrical, phytomorphic and occasionally ornitomorphic and zoomorphic designs, similar to the designs used in tapestry. It may be fringed with a thin wool–yarn, one colour woven band or a band called *"wincha"* which is woven with the "small comb" technique.

Occasionally one may find a flat plaited band.

The other difference is its place on the saddle since it has the functions of a *matra* a *ristro* and a *jergón*. It is an ornamented piece, and the user likes to show it.

Caronilla from Mendoza (both sides)

Caronillas with floral decoration

Claudio Gay (1800–1873) "Chilean Peons"

Cojinillos

*P. Pueyrredón
(1823–1870)
"A break in the
country"*

*Mota and chilla
Cojinillo
(plush and threads)*

"*Cojinillo or Pellón: piece that is placed on the encimeras
(piece of leather which has been stamped into patterns with
a hot iron and which is placed on the seat of the saddle) and
the bastos (the saddle itself; it is made of wood, with a peak
before and behind, or in many cases nothing but two rolls
lying one along each side of the back of the horse) to make
the saddle more comfortable. It can be a woollen or a cotton
blanket, or a sheepskin with all its wool. The cojinillo is the
mattress of the gaucho's bed.*". (Saubidet)

Out of comfort or as a luxury, this piece has always
been carefully chosen by traditionalists as well as
rural workers.

The *cojinillo de pellón* or simply *pellón*, is made of
sheepskin big enough to cover the saddle. The skins
differ greatly, the skins of Criolla and Lincoln sheep

have long wisps but the Criolla has coarse, straight hair, the Lincoln has silky, shining hair, which, although it is beautiful, its wool is not the best. They do not get matted and form a pad so they have to be supplemented with another one and need frequent brushing.

The best ones according to Justo P. Sáenz, are the black face sheep, also called "of rounded wool", with a compact mass of wool that gives the *cojinillo* elasticity and consistency.

*Mota and chilla
Cojinillo
(plush and threads)*

Once the skin has been chosen, one has to wash the wool carefully and it has to be kneaded. This last procedure is essential.

But the very best *cojinillo*, used by the rich gaucho was the *cojinillo* made of cotton thread. It did not replace the sheepskin *cojinillo* but it was its complement, the sheepskin is comfortable, the *cojinillo* made of thread is beautiful.

Where did the first thread *cojinillos* come from?

The most famous ones come from Tucumán, they are dark blue, white (made of natural wool) and black and were woven with goat hair.

*Mota and chilla
Cojinillo
(plush and threads)*

They were very expensive, because it did not pay the work of the weaver.

When the English started supplying the gauchos with all the elements that he needed, the *cojinillos* were very well imitated in Manchester and Birmingham, and flooded the market of Buenos Aires and its neighbouring region.

The Araucano Indians of the eighteenth century and beginnings of the nineteenth century used the *cojinillo* with *mota* and *chilla*. *Mota* (tight curl or crinkly hair) is the name given to the central part of the *cojinillo*, which looks like a plushy carpet and *chilla* are the borders with ten to fifteen centimetre long tassels.

Thread cojinillo

They are usually dark blue, black, and natural white and resemble the *chañuntukos* the Mapuche Indians used on the other side of the Andes.

The technique is the same, the tassels are directly woven as tufts on the weft and the *mota* is formed with threads of wool tightly attached to the warp by means of the *ghiordës* knot.

The *chañuntukos* were thinner than the *mota* and *chilla cojinillos*, usually black, with spaced tassels, because they were born as bottom blankets. When they started being used on the saddle, they were changed; they got the long tassels and colours and designs were added in Chile and other Andean Argentine regions.

Chilla Cojinillo with wool without spinning

The wool for the thread came from a breed of a sheep crossed with a goat, the famous Pampa sheep, now extinguished.

Different techniques were used to weave and make the tassels of a *cojinillo*.

The best way was to weave and fix the threads at the same time is with the *matra* technique, with four borders, without tassels or hems. As with everything, the market fixed the production rules.

J. Daufresne "Indian family", 1844

When both the demand and the prize went up, the weavers started to weave the basic part without the four–border technique but with the poncho technique, with tassels on both ends, finished off with a flat plait. This system helped the weavers save time and the *cojinillos* looked like those woven with the four–border technique, because the tassels covered the borders.

Later on they started using just any woven piece that could be found.

The only require-
ment was the right
measurements and
the dark colour.

They sewed the
hems on the four
borders and fixed
the threads (thinly
spun and twisted,
taking good care
that the material

*C. Morel
(1813–1894)
"The gaucho and his
apparel"*

should be of good quality) following the family tradition, the experience or imagination of the weaver.
They had to make sure that the tassels were firmly
fixed.

There are *cojinillos* with vertical knots, following
the line of the warp, or horizontal knots accompany-
ing the direction of the weft, threads used individu-
ally or taken in bundles of four or five, with or
without knots, etc.

The characteristic of old *cojinillos* is the direction of
the weaving, the lines of the warp follow the central
axis, like the Araucanian *matras*, the ponchos, the
sashes, etc. and the reason is that the warp has to support the tension the piece usually undergoes.

The English *cojinillos* differ from the native ones,
not only in the basic part but in the way the threads
were fixed.

The warp crosses the axis of the piece, and the
threads accompany the weft and emerge after crossing the warp several times. They practically make up
the weft of the basic part.

*Mota and chilla
cojinillo with spun
wool (plush and
threads)*

Llicllas and Awayos

They are rectangular garments formed by two cloths sewn in the centre, ornamented with *pallai* or stripes along their sides and in the central part, at both sides of the central seam.

They are approximately 1 m long or a bit wider, but their dimensions vary according to the user, which can even be a small girl.

The Spanish priest Bernabé Cobo (1582–1657) wrote about the *lliclla* "they put it on the shoulders, and they make both ends meet on their breast where it is attached with a pin. These are their shawls, which reach their legs. They take it off while working and while they are at home."

When he says pin he is referring to the "*tupus or tupos*", pieces of metal, mainly of silver, made of a long needle with a sharpened end to pin their garments together and having a round ornament on the other end.

The Araucano Indians adopted the round–tipped tupo and the variety of a sphere which was called acucha (corruption of the Spanish word aguja, needle). The Spanish conquerors called it punch.

Sometimes they have the form of a spoon, which has been chiselled and engraved.

Licllas and *awayos* are the same garment. *lliclla* is the Aymara name, *awayo* the Quechua name.

Tari, similar to the awayo, woven in one piece and related to the coca ceremony.

The *awayo* is still being used as a garment in the Argentine and Bolivian Altiplano, it is also used to carry provisions, clothes and household tools and as a blanket to carry their babies on the back.

This system of carrying babies was started being used in the nineteenth century. Up to the eighteenth century, the kids were carried in a basket as if it were a cradle.

They can be woven with alpaca hair, sheep's wool, llama hair and with cotton, sometimes mixing these materials in the same piece.

They are woven with many different designs and finished with different sorts of fringes, woven in the same piece.

In many *awayos*, one half has the same colours as the other one, but the *pallai* differs. They are items of the dowry and each piece contains the designs of the regions the bride and the bridegroom come from.

Felipe Guamán Poma de Ayala "Indians with tupo", 1587

Sashes

Sash is called "huaca" in Aymara, "chumpi" in Quechua and "tra-rihue" in Mapuche.

The sash, called *faja* in Spanish, has been used since time immemorial. Used as a support of the garment around the waist or to encircle longer dresses, it has been used by both men and women. It is still used in military uniforms, in ecclesiastical habits and in the attire of rich and poor.

Excellent pre–Hispanic fabrics that show the ability of our ancestors can be admired in many private collections and museums.

Sashes from the south

Detail of the sash of the Angualasto mummy, Etnographic Museum, Juan B. Ambrosetti, (1200–1400 AD)

Plain weave silk sash from the south

*Tubular pampa sash
(complementary warp)*

Sashes from the North

Wool sash woven with the small–comb technique

In the northern area, in pre–Hispanic times, sashes were used exclusively by women. They started being used by men in the eighteenth century because of the influence of the Spanish fashion and after the prohibition to use Indian garments after the uprising in 1781.

The term sash is called *huaca* in Aymara and *chumpi* in Quechua.

It is said that the poncho was used with a sash as belt around the waist, which is still done in Potosí in the twentieth century. It is logical that this happened, because the poncho substituted the *unku*, the pre–Inca shirt which was nothing but a poncho sewn along the borders to close the sides, leaving the slits open to pass the arms through, so when the poncho replaced the *unku*, it was tightened along the waist by means of a sash, to have a garment that would have the same functions.

In the Argentine northwest the sashes are made using the plain weave technique, have only one colour, with stripes or "small comb". In the province of Jujuy, due to Bolivian influence, the sashes are woven with double face, Andean pattern band and complementary warp techniques.

The techniques used in Peru and the Bolivian Altiplano are so varied that each community or ethnic group has a distinctive features that distinguish their sashes.

Sheep's wool, cameloid hair (mainly alpaca), cotton and the combination of them have been used.

The size of the sashes differs from place to place. Some are 4 or 5 m long, generally woven with pattern bands using the double face technique, and there are others that are not longer than 1 m called "tightners" which can be either tubular or with pattern bands.

The width also varies, from 10 cm down to 2 or 3 cm, as those used in the Calcha region, which are 2 or 3 m long pattern band sashes with flower designs.

In Peru and Bolivia tubular woollen sashes may be found, the designs copy natural motifs, not only phytomorphic, but zoomorphic and ornitomorphic motifs as well. They can also have geometrical designs and the form of human beings (anthropomorphic).

As with all textile techniques, the complex double face fabrics, tubular and pattern band with complementary warp, were born in this area and spread later on along the Andean corridor until they reached the Chilean south and then crossed the Andes to be woven by Mapuche and Pampa Indians in Argentina.

Wool sash from Cuyo

Sash from Alto Peru, (detail)

The horse patterns appeared after the arrival of the Spaniards

Sashes from the South

Leaving aside the sashes that were created for other purposes, such as boot garters and hair bands, the sashes in the south were created with the flat plait method. Later on the technique was used only for garters, and then, eventually, they were abandoned.

The sashes of the south may be divided in Pampa sashes (tubular), Araucanian or pattern band sashes (double face with complementary warp) and Mapuche sashes (false double face, supplementary warp, like the *matras*).

The most famous ones are the first two, especially because they are difficult to make, but there are also important and beautiful Mapuche sashes.

Pampa Sashes

These sashes were woven in vertical looms, and for the warps, two 40 cm long posts of *colihue (Nothofagus dombeyi)* wood were staked into the ground. The separation between one and the other depended on the length of the piece to be woven (generally 2 to 3 m). The weaver used two other sticks to separate the threads of the warp.

Then she started walking around the warp, as if it were a ritual dance carrying the endless threads from one end to the other, sometimes in silence, and sometimes humming very old songs that have been transmitted for centuries, from mothers to daughters.

Generally, these sashes had two contrasting colours, to clearly show the double face cloth. Occasionally they added a third and even a forth colour which could either form part of the border or of one or both faces of the piece. Traditionally they chose white, yellow, black, red and dark blue, but without rejecting the other colours.

The name given to this type of loom was "small sticks loom" or "small boards loom" because the work is prepared putting the sticks one after the other to mark the design, which are then taken away as the crossing of the weft takes place.

This Pampa technique produces a tubular fabric, practically two bands, one on top of the other, one colour each and linked only along the borders. A hand could be put into this sort of sleeve if, when weaving, the threads would not pass from one side to the other and vice versa.

The proof of the existence of these Pampa sashes is given by Enrique Kermes in 1893. He writes about the fabrics made of spun wool: *"These fabrics were made by the Indians for their own private use, for the men: ponchos, chiripáes and sashes to hold the latter. These sashes were 3 to 6 cm wide, and 2 to 3 m long. For them to last longer, they were made in a special form. They are woven with two complete warp assemblies that form two separate fabrics, the link between them is obtained when the threads of one warp pass to the other (when they are needed) to form the design. The designs of these sashes turn up in both sides but with different alternate colours."*

This also helps to prove the authenticity of the Pampa girth, used to fasten the *cojinillo* to the saddle which were used to enhance the elegance of a beautiful saddle.

In general, the designs were traditional geometrical ornaments that imitate the tie warp design of the poncho.

This is a modern adaptation of what is called Pampa pattern, also seen in simple sashes made with the plain weave and *ikat* techniques.

Araucanian Sashes

The technique used to make *trarihues*, sashes in Mapuche language, is called Andean technique. It is double faced, with complementary warp, with important Incan influence. There are modern *trarihues* that do not respect the intricate rules of the Araucanian weavers' tradition, that is, they can have just any sort of design, not without beauty in some cases, but if we speak of antique *trarihues*, then they can be classified in the same way ponchos are classified.

The word *trarihue* means "woman's sash", but they have been worn by men, especially those that are nowadays interested in keeping old traditions.

Men's sashes called *trarichiripa*, are items of a much simple manufacture, they are red in its basic structure, the study of which has been practically impossible. They are difficult to find because the Mapuche Indians used them to tie their *chiripá* and they stopped using the *chiripá* a long time ago.

The *pollki–trarihue* is a sash with interrupted or segmented, longitudinal stripes. The *wirin–trarihue*, has continuous longitudinal central lines and the *wisiwel–trarihue* has diagonal designs.

The *ñimin–trarihue* deserves a special description. It is an item that is profusely ornamented with symbols. The border is divided into five sectors, each with a different meaning.

All the *ñimin–trarihues* are similar in their central part, the colours are invariably red or black on a white basis, and the design is always the same: *Lukutuel*, the man or woman knelt in a religious ceremony. They are represented in a very peculiar way.

Araucanian sash

Detail of a pollki–trarihue

Where does *Lukutuel* come from? The researchers think it is unique in the world. The human figure has been cut into two and unfolded in various directions.

Taking *Lukutuel* as the pattern, and through a process of re–elaboration, it was used to represent other designs, for instance *Rayén* (the flower) and *Temu*, the magic tree that gives to the water that flows beside it, the gift of a healthy life to new born children whose eyes have been washed with it.

In the centre of the *trarihue*, flows a long story that narrates ancestral events, expressions of desires, and other legends of tribal origin.

Trarihue

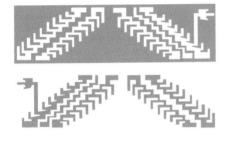

Kai–kai, negative force
Treng–treng, positive force

Rayén, flower

Lukutuel, kneeled prayer

Temu, tree

Detail of Lukutuel y Temu

Mapuche Sashes

These sashes are usually woven in the same looms used by the Mapuche Indians for their ponchos and *matras*. For their ornamentation they use the technique of supplementary warp. The designs are the same used in the *matras* and in the bands of their ponchos and they usually follow the design of the geometrical rhombuses.

The material used is sheep's wool and the colours may be white or natural with brown designs, or natural, without dye, together with other bright colours used in the same piece.

In general, all sashes used in Argentina and Chile are 2 to 3 m long and have a width of 6 to 10 cm, the only exception being the sashes from Jujuy, with Andean pattern band technique which are shorter (up to 1,50 m).

Mapuche sash woven with false double face

Toba Indian woollen sash woven with weft–face technique

Otras fajas

In the Chaco region, we can find sashes made of wool, in the same way they are made in the northwest, but the most characteristic ones are those made of caraguatá or chaguá fibres, pretty, but without any special hand-made value.

Some aboriginal communities in the Chaco, as for instance the tobas, weave curious weft faced sashes. Similar sashes are woven with the same technique in Mendoza.

R. Ramos
"Нuecuvu Мapu"
1993

Blankets

Chamal

B. Panunzi
"Country people"

O. Heffer Bissett
"Indian spinning"

The *chamal* is an item woven in a loom, it has a rectangular form, and its dimensions vary (approximately 1,40 by 1,20 m).

The Mapuche women used it as dress, holding it with a *tupo* or an *akucha* using a sash around their waist. Men carried it at the waist and they folded it in a special way. The *chamal* used by women is called *kepam*, the one used by men is called *chiripá*.

Both were woven in only one piece with warp face technique, with four borders and using only one colour, predominantly black for the *kepam* and brownish colours for the *chiripá*.

Later on, the gaucho adopted the black *chiripá* made of merino wool as an elegant garment, covering the long white *calzoncillos* (sort of trousers), which were finished with fine tassels, embroidered and which reached the gauchos boots. The pictures of gauchos in the nineteenth century show so many different designs of *chiripá*, that a classification of them is practically impossible. Many were adaptations of ponchos woven in fine wool, usually from the Alto Peru, and even industrial ponchos brought from England.

The form to wear a *chiripá* is the following: Two sides of the rectangular cloth are put around the waist, holding them with the hand against the stomach.

The other hand brings the other part that is hanging at the back forward between the legs, putting it together at the waist. Everything is then fixed with a sash.

Anonimous after William Mac Cann, "Peasant from Buenos Aires"

Pontro

The pontro is the Mapuche blanket. It is woven in the same way as the *chamal*, with the only difference that the piece has to be heavy.

The thick thread wool is tightly woven. The usual designs are stripes of different colours and they may have pompoms in the corners.

They are between 1,40 and 1,90 m long by about the same size or bigger.

Puyo or Cama

Pullo is the blanket used in the north. In the northwest, they are woven in two pieces and they have a hem. In the Alto Peru they used the four border technique to weave them.

They are ornamented with many designs. They can have stripes of different colours, simple pattern bands made with the "small comb" technique. Sometimes all three techniques are used in one item.

Puyo

Bedspreads

The most beautiful, colourful and varied bedspreads were made up to the twentieth century in Catamarca and Santiago del Estero. These are items woven with warp–faced–cloth technique in one or two pieces. These pieces are designed using different techniques such as brocade (threads that belong to the woven cloth, but are only seen when the threads "design"), *bordo* (see p 118), with flowers, zoomorphic and geometrical designs, often all of them together. In others, the technique of weft cloth is used, like tapestry, with the same ornaments.

Embroided blanket from Santiago del Estero woven in two pieces. The field is woven with a warp–face technique.

The edges have Spanish style fringes in three or in four borders. Some have pompoms, all around tassels, flat plaits and even band tassels of pre–Columbian influence.

Today there are bedspreads made of wool dyed in bright colours with bands made with the "small comb" technique and all around fringes.

Bedspread of Santiago del Estero with geometrical designs

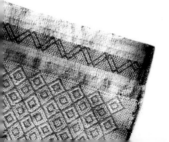

Detail of a Santiago del Estero bedspread woven with warp–face technique and ornamented with bands of "small–comb" technique

Rugs

The old rugs from the south were woven with the same warp face technique used by the Mapuche Indians for their textile craft. These rugs were produced with the techniques used for saddle blankets, ponchos and sashes.

Emeric Essex Vidal (1791–1861) "Santo Domingo church"

Lamas

Mapuche Indian selling rugs

Lama is the name given by the Mapuche Indians to the rugs and they are, with logical modifications to their domestic use, copies of rural pieces. Pedro Mege Rosso interprets them as the expression of a precise symbolic language.

The design techniques used are warp–ikat (similar to those used in ponchos but with brighter colours), pattern bands with supplementary warp or false double face (as the technique used in *matras* but with warp tassels) and pattern bands with complementary warp or double face.

The rugs woven today are generally with pattern bands of false double face, with similar designs as those used in *matras* and *fajas*.

Choapinos

The *choapino* is called *chañuntuku* in Chile. It is an item woven with four borders with a finish of plush or curls, depending on the type of thread used. The yarn is tied to the warp in different ways; the most common one is the *ghiordës* knot, also called *gueurdes*. The threads that have been tied are cut at the same height, around two or three centimetres to form the plush. The borders of the cloth are left untied to attach some threads that will form a tasselled fringe. These yarns are woven directly from the weft.

Choapino designed with plush and mota

There are some that are completely covered by threads lightly twisted, and sometimes with a tuft of wool directly tied to the warp. Those are called "*de chilla*", as the cojinillo.

Although the *choapino* was born as a *pelero*, and then it was used as a *cojinillo* on the saddle, its softness led its user take it home and use it, for a certain time at the beginning, and then definitively, as rug or as a blanket for his favourite armchair.

The most traditional colours are black, blue and natural, because they are the colours of the *cojinillos*, but other colours are also found in old pieces, some with designs made by the threads of the plush.

Other rugs from the South

There are rugs which are totally covered by plush called "*de chilla*". The name derives from the Pampa sheep, which were called that way. The wool used for the plush is spun wool; the thread dyed beforehand, is tied with practically no twisting.

Some rugs have the threads cut as if it were plush and others keep the yarn uncut. The finishing then is very irregular, similar to the chilla *chañuntukus*.

As a rule they are made with natural coloured wool, white, grey and some shades of brown. Generally those of the nineteenth century are so colourful that they look like the works of modern tapestry artists.

Small chilla rug

Small plush rug

Rug with false double face decoration

Rugs from the North and the Centre

Rugs any size or form may be found in this region, from the small rug that the servant carried for the lady to kneel down in church to the very big ones that covered the lady's rooms or the floor of the church.

At the beginning, the techniques and designs were copied from the rugs brought from Europe, because the religious orders were in charge of the teaching in the monasteries, but later on, the *criollo* weavers introduces new ornaments, such as those used in wall–hangings.

Detail of a bordo rug

The Italian naturalist Clemente Onelli (1864–1924) researched Argentine textile handicraft and founded in 1918 in Córdoba a school of textiles and rugs, where he tried to spread the art of bordo. He did the same in Tucumán and started a workshop in Parque de los Patricios in the city of Buenos Aires.

Clara Díaz
"The cocks of Father Fierro", 1987
2m x 2,1m

Clara Díaz
"Beetles and
Laoconts", 1984
2m x 2,1m

Several techniques were used, in general they were woven with the balanced cloth technique with flat embroidery, warp faced fabrics with plush were made with the ghiordës knot covering the whole surface (with or without a tasselled fringe, applied or structural) and warp or weft face cloth with brocade and bordo ornaments.

In Santiago del Estero mainly brocade was woven, whereas in Córdoba, Tucumán, Salta, La Rioja and Catamarca, the plush techniques flourished.

It is worth visiting the weavers' schools in San Luis and Catamarca where large, beautiful pieces are produced, mainly for institutions not only from Argentina but from foreign countries as well.

Bordo is a very old technique, which reached its peak in colonial times in the provinces of Córdoba and Tucumán. This technique is not woven in the classical loom but embroidered on a balanced wool or vegetable fibre cloth, such as hessian or canvas. Works of art have been created using this technique as from the sixteenth century on, as those made by the famous Clara Díaz in Córdoba today.

The bordo technique is started by designing ornaments on the canvas. Then the background (the part that will not be covered with bordo) is embroidered with cross–stitches or cock's–feet stitches. Then from the centre to the borders, wool threads are passed by means of a needle, which are then tied to a piece of wire. When the wire is removed, uniform curls are left. The name of this technique derives from the Spanish word bordar (to embroid).

*Tulumba rug of the
province of Córdoba.
Plush technique,
threads tied with
ghiordës knot.*

Wall–hangings

Wall–hanging from San Salvador, Jujuy

The wall–hangings from the south are practically inexistent, and the pieces available today are just produced for tourists using traditional designs made with the double face technique. Frequently, in the catalogues of the Argentine and Chilean artisans, the *matras* are called "murals".

The real native tapestry was born in the provinces of the northwest and the centre of Argentina and it derives, as the rugs did, from European models.

Sapagua, petroglyphs

Wall–hangings are produced with the warp face technique (used in oriental kelim as in European gobelin in vertical looms with or without heddles in frames called semi–looms. In both cases, the thin warp threads, generally made of cotton, are set so wide apart that the weft packs down between them and completely covers the warp.

The threads of the warp can be fixed by means of nails stuck on the frame to keep a uniform separation, pass through dents on the frame, or they can be tied in the same way as for the four–border system to weave with the warp face technique.

Wall–hanging from Salta

In pre–Hispanic times, previous to the Inca Empire, the weft face technique was used to weave tapestry and garments, leaving sometimes the weft threads when the colour is changed, producing a cloth with natural buttonholes.

The arrival of the Spaniards brought a deep change in the manufacture of tapestry because the missionaries introduced European techniques and designs.

Urn, Santa María culture

Wall–hanging from the north with European designs, nineteenth century

The Indians immediately learnt from the missionaries to copy classical designs of European tapestry, including works of great the masters, fusing the weaving of tapestry and the manufacture of rugs. Motifs from heraldic shields were included in the decoration that hung from the balconies of the most influential families.

After the declaration of independence, convents and monasteries kept the designs and techniques. The weavers, those who did not belong to the higher social classes, gave birth to the wall–hangings that really represent our country. Only conditioned by the basic technique, they started copying scenes of everyday life: landscapes, flowers, animals and people. They were inspired by their observation of, for instance, people carrying firewood, weaving, modelling in clay, etc.

The petroglyphs in Sapagua, near Humahuaca, those in Cerro Colorado, not far from Yavi, both in the province of Jujuy also attracted the attention of the weavers as well as the archeological finds of pre–Columbian cultures such as Santa María, Belén and Aguada, (province of Catamarca), and Candelaria, (province of Tucumán) and wove them in their wall hangings.

Wall–hanging from Neuquen

Today, the weavers design not only these classical patterns, which are repeated with certain varieties of colour and forms, but they also include motifs of their own inspiration. Real works of art and excellent abstract compositions can no longer be classified as handicraft.

An example of this is given by the members of the Cruz family. Their works can be admired in the Museum at the site of the Quilmes ruins, near Amaicha del Valle, in the province of Tucumán. There, they have started a vigorous cultural undertaking.

Pieces woven with the traditional warp face technique have interested urban artisans but because of their worldwide diffusion, tapestries have aroused the interest of visual art creators.

From the Argentine Jacques Larochette on, an offspring of a family of tapestry weavers from the famous Aubusson factory, with his workshop in Bariloche (province of Río Negro) in 1948, to the whirlwind of artists that emerged in the sixties who adopted mixed techniques with European inspiration and special designs from artists such as Berni, Polesello, Soldi, Chab, Pérez Célis, and Alonso (contemporary Argentine painters), Argentine tapestry artist have gained an important place in art shows

S. Trigos
"Megaflower"

The work of Silke
and Silvina Trigos
are an example of the
excellent level
achieved by tapestry
artists in Argentina.

Silke
"The Devil"
1993

and have crossed the frontiers to achieve fame in important international exhibitions.

"Tapestries have abandoned the wall", is what art catalogues repeat, and that is exactly the idea of the three–dimensional structure adopted by these works of art that have left the prison of the frame and the fibres, imposed by tradition.

Randa and Ñandutí

Ñandutí mantilla

Altough these crafts are not made with a loom or any weaving technique, they form part of the old handicrafts made in Argentina.

The technique used in making *randas*, brought by the Spanish religious orders are still used in the provinces of Salta, Catamarca, Tucumán, Santiago del Estero and Córdoba.

It is very similar to lace and it has replaced it for centuries in napkins, curtains and dresses.

For making a *randa* a net is prepared with a needle and cotton thread no 200. The eye of the mesh is measured with the help of a small stick. Once the net is finished, it is placed in the frame and the artisan starts embroidering with cotton threads of different thickness according to the design.

The best *randas* come from El Cercado, a village in the province of Tucumán.

Clementi Onelli wrote in 1916:

Randa

"The lace from Tucumán is not only fashionable but it is of noble ancestry. It is of noble ancestry because it was started and taught by the nuns of the convent in Lima. Although its origin belongs to the Christian education, the randa was apparently misused. Nuns, priests and bishops disapproved of the randa. It was only logical since the ladies from Lima at the time of the viceroyalty were a little bit more daring than the ladies today: wide

silken skirts, that reached at least two fingers above the knees (I say above), and from there, down to the ankle, rich and transparent randa, produced in the convents of the chaste nuns."

Although the material used for the ñandutí is cotton, in the province of Corrientes wool, raffia and vegetable fibres such as pita and coconut thread are used.

The term *ñandutí* derives from the Guaraní word *landute* (spider), and it is a craft that has a strong relationship with the web of a spider because it starts from a centre and then it extends in the style of a web. This technique came from Paraguay and then spread into the Argentine provinces of Formosa, Chaco, Misiones, Santa Fe, Entre Ríos and especially to the province of Corrientes, where it became rooted and where the artisans have created excellent pieces.

To make a *ñandutí*, a balanced cloth with loose warp and weft is woven in a loom or semi–loom (frame) and designs are embroidered on it. Once the work is finished, the basic cloth is cut away with the help of small scissors.

Randa

Today there are a variety of ways of mounting the threads on which the designs are going to be embroidered: 1. On a small cushion, some pins are stuck forming the outer border of the craft and from there, the threads will cross the cushion forming the reticule. 2. A fine piece of cloth is put on a frame and the threads, crossing the cloth, are fixed to it along the border. 3. On round or square pieces of cardboard with indented borders, the threads are tied. When the work is finished, the thread assembly is taken off the cardboard. This last technique is the easiest one, and is the way the girls are taught to make a *ñandutí*.

Textiles and design

Nowadays, traditional fabrics are used, not only as exhibition objects but as decorative items as well. The fashion now is to use them in upholstery, dresses and fashion accessories.

This tendency, although it seems to be a bit irreverent, because the pieces are not used for what they were made for, implies the positive idea that Argentine handmade handicrafts can be part of everyday life. They can carry warmth and beauty, and the history of the sons of the earth, narrated by the diligent and swift hands of the weavers.

Upholstery with Argentine textiles

Bibliography

BARTH, Kathy: *Viajando por Bolivia a través de las Maravillas del Tejido,* Bolivia, 2001.

BURGOS, Fausto: *Tejidos Incaicos y Criollos,* Buenos Aires, 1927.

CERVELLINO, G. Miguel: *El tejido Mapuche. Proceso del Hilado, Tejido y Teñido en Base a Colorantes Vegetales Chilenos,* Santiago de Chile, 1877

COBO, Bernabé, *Historia del Nuevo Mundo,* Madrid, 1956.

Chertudi S, Nardi R.: *Tejidos araucanos en la Argentina,* Buenos Aires, 1962.

DE LA VEGA, Garcilaso: *Comentarios Reales,* Lisboa, 1609.

D'ÓRBIGNY, Alcide: *Viaje por América Meridional,* Buenos Aires: Emecé, 1999.

ESSEX VIDAL, Emeric: *Picturesque Illustrations of Buenos Ayres and Monte Video,* Buenos Aires: Emecé, 1999.

FLORES OCHOA, J.: *Clasificación y Nominación de los Camélidos Sudamericanos, La Tecnología en el Mundo Andino,* Méjico, 1981.

FURLONG, Guillermo: *Arte en el Río de la Plata,* Buenos Aires, 1993.

GISBERT, Teresa: *Arte Textil y Mundo Andino,* La Paz, 1987.

GRESLEBIN, Héctor: *Introducción al Estudio del Arte Autóctono de la América del Sur,* Buenos Aires, 1958.

GROUSSAC, Paul: *Anales de la Biblioteca, Apéndice Documental,* Buenos Aires, 1915.

HUAMAN POMA DE AYALA: Felipe, *Nueva Crónica y Buen Gobierno,* Paris: Institut D'Ethnologie, 1936.

INSTITUTO NACIONAL DE ANTROPOLOGÍA: *1000 Años de Tejido en la Argentina,* Buenos Aires, 1978.

JOSEPH, Claude: «Los Tejidos Araucanos», *Revista Universitaria de Chile,* Santiago de Chile, 1931.

KERMES, Enrique: «Tejidos Pampas», *Revista del Jardín Zoológico de Buenos Ayres,* Buenos Aires, 1893.

MAC CANN, William: *Viaje a Caballo por las Provincias Argentinas,* Buenos Aires: Solar, 1969.

MEGE ROSSO, Pedro: *Arte Textil Mapuche,* Santiago de Chile, 1990.

MARÍ, Jorge et al.: *El Apero Criollo,* Buenos Aires: Vega y Eguiguren, 2000.

MILLAN DE PALAVECINO, María Delia: *El Poncho, estudio etnográfico,* Buenos Aires, 1954.

——————: *Area de Expansión del Tejido Araucano,* 1964.

MONTECINO, Sonia: *Mujeres de la Tierra,* Chile, 1984.

PAUCKE, Florian: *Hacia allá y para acá. Una estada entre los indios Mocobíes, (1749–1767),* Buenos Aires: Instituto de

Antropología de la Universidad Nacional de Tucumán, 1942.

SAENZ, Justo P. (h.), *Equitación Gaucha*, Buenos Aires: Peuser, 1959.

SAUBIDET, Tito: *Vocabulario y Refranero Criollo*, Buenos Aires: Editorial Claire, 1978.

SCHMIEDL, Ulrico: *Viaje al Río de la Plata*, Buenos Aires: Emecé, 1997.

SILVA SANTISTEBAN, Fernando: *Los obrajes en el Virreinato del Perú*, Lima, 1964.

STRAMIGIOLI, Celestina: *Teñido con Colorantes Vegetales*, Buenos Aires: Galerna, 1991.

TARANTO, Enrique, Marí Jorge: *Textiles de Uso Tradicional*, Buenos Aires: Asociación Criolla Argentina, 2001.

TAULLARD, Alfredo: *Tejidos y Ponchos Indígenas de Sudamérica*, Buenos Aires: Guillermo Kraft, 1949.

TERRERA, Alfredo: *El Caballo Criollo en la Tradición Argentina*, Buenos Aires, 1969.

VILÁ, Bibiana: *Camellos sin Joroba*, Buenos Aires: Colihue, 2001

ZEBALLOS, Estanislao S.: *Viaje al País de los Araucanos*, Buenos Aires: Solar, 1994.

Martinez Compañón,
(1735–1797)
"Indio del Purap"

Index

Illustrations are set in bold

Martinez Compañón,
(1735–1797)
"Español a caballo"
e "India pastora"

Audubon

Leslie Mihordin
7716 Rio Estrada Way
Sacramento, CA 95831-4461

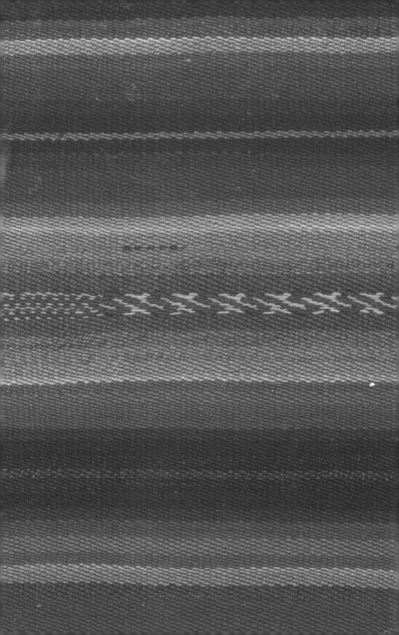